New Psalms
from the Old Psalms

Real Conversations with God

WILLIAM G. HENDERSON, JR.

© 2019
Published in the United States by Nurturing Faith Inc., Macon GA,
www.nurturingfaith.net.

Library of Congress Cataloging-in-Publication Data is available.

ISBN 978-1-63528-061-6

All scripture quotations and sources are taken from THE HOLY BIBLE, NEW INTERNATIONAL VERSION. Copyright 1973, 1978, 1984 International Bible Society. Used by permission of Zondervan Bible Publishers.

All hymn titles and quotations are taken from the *Baptist Hymnal.* Copyright 2008 LifeWay Worship. Used by reference of Public Domain Hymns.

Illustrations by Margaret Levy Mullis. Charleston, South Carolina. Used by permission.

All rights reserved. Printed in the United States of America

Contents

Foreword 1

Book One: Psalms 1–41

Psalm 1 4
  God Holds the Secret of
  True Happiness

Psalm 2 4
  Proclaiming God's Rule

Psalm 3 5
  Beaten Down, I Shall Rise

Psalm 4 5
  A Bedtime Prayer

Psalm 5 6
  It's a Jungle Out There!

Psalm 6 6
  Exhausted, I Cry and Pray

Psalm 7 7
  I Am at Wit's End!

Psalm 8 7
  I Am Amazed at God!

Psalm 9 8
  I Am Gloriously Happy!

Psalm 10 8
  An Evil Man Is Torturing Us!
  Save Us!

Psalm 11 9
  It Is Scary Trying to Do Right!

Psalm 12 10
  It Is Lonely at the Top!

Psalm 13 10
  I'm Just Struggling

Psalm 14 10
  Where Have All the Good
  People Gone?

Psalm 15 11
  Who Is Good Enough to See God?

Psalm 16 11
  So Much to Be Thankful For!

Psalm 17 12
  Troubles Give Way to Trust! I'll
  See God!

Psalm 18 12
  God Is Faithful and Beautiful!

Psalm 19 14
  Living Words Are Everywhere

Psalm 20 14
  A Prayer for My Friends

Psalm 21 15
  Our God Is a Winner!

Psalm 22 16
  Despair!

Psalm 23 17
  His Shepherding Love

Psalm 24 17
  The Lord, Strong and Mighty!

Psalm 25 18
  Forgive Me, Lord

Psalm 26 19
  Test Me—Try Me

Psalm 27 19
  God Never Fails

Psalm 28 20
  Calling on the Lord

Psalm 29 20
  Worship Like It's Supposed to Be

Psalm 30 21
  Why We Praise Him

Psalm 31 21
Words for Worship

Psalm 32 22
All About Forgiveness

Psalm 33 23
God Has Plans

Psalm 34 23
Praise, Praise, and Practice!

Psalm 35 24
Battling with God as My Helper

Psalm 36 25
A Message to This World

Psalm 37 26
Never, Never, Never Quit!

Psalm 38 27
Sometimes I Goof Up, God

Psalm 39 28
I Want Out!

Psalm 40 28
Swallowed Up in Troubles

Psalm 41 29
The Great Physician

Book Two: Psalms 42–72

Psalm 42 32
There Is a Hunger Within

Psalm 43 33
Send the Light

Psalm 44 33
You're in Charge, Though Sometimes It's Hard!

Psalm 45 34
A Wedding Song

Psalm 46 35
Never Fear; God Is Here

Psalm 47 36
God Is Great; God Is Good!

Psalm 48 36
Great God! Check Him Out at Church!

Psalm 49 37
It's God, Not Your Money, You Fool!

Psalm 50 38
Looking for a Thankful Heart

Psalm 51 39
Mercy Trumps Punishment

Psalm 52 40
The Young and the Restless

Psalm 53 41
Yes, God Is Still There!

Psalm 54 41
Enemies on My Left, God on My Right!

Psalm 55 42
A Single Plea for Help

Psalm 56 43
Another Plea for Help

Psalm 57 43
Great Is the Lord!

Psalm 58 44
Hot Is My Anger

Psalm 59 44
Deliverance

Psalm 60 45
There Is No Winning Without the Lord

Psalm 61 45
Lead Me to the Rock

Psalm 62 46
In God Alone

Psalm 63 46
Streams in the Desert

Psalm 64 47
God Will Avenge

Psalm 65 48
Wonderful, Wonderful God!

Psalm 66 49
Wonder of Wonders

Psalm 67 50
May God Bless Us

Psalm 68 50
Rise Up, O Lord

Psalm 69 52
He Will Make the Weak Strong

Psalm 70 53
Quickly, Lord!

Psalm 71 53
I am Growing Old; Keep Me Close

Psalm 72 54
God's Special Leader

Book Three: Psalms 73–89

Psalm 73 58
False Religion

Psalm 74 59
Gone Are the Sacred Retreats!

Psalm 75 60
God Always Has the Final Word

Psalm 76 61
God Rules the Nations

Psalm 77 61
God Is Great, and God Is Always Good

Psalm 78 62
A List of God's Works

Psalm 79 66
When God Is Angry, Nobody Wins

Psalm 80 67
We Call Upon the Lord, Our God

Psalm 81 67
Because God Can Make a Way

Psalm 82 68
Hear Ye! Hear Ye! Court Is Now in Session!

Psalm 83 69
Holy Silence Doesn't Cut It

Psalm 84 69
There's No Better Place Than the Church

Psalm 85 70
Welcome Back, Sons and Daughters

Psalm 86 71
What Becomes of the Broken-Hearted?

Psalm 87 72
God Chose the Church

Psalm 88 73
Depression

Psalm 89 74
O God, Remember the Covenant

Book Four: Psalms 90–106

Psalm 90 78
An Ancient Reflection and Prayer

Psalm 91 79
Close to Thee, Close to Thee

Psalm 92 80
How Great Is Our God

Psalm 93 81
Endless Praise

Psalm 94 81
We Shall Overcome Some Day

Psalm 95 83
With the Voice of Singing
Psalm 96 84
God Is the Mighty King of Love
Psalm 97 84
Lord of All the Earth
Psalm 98 85
The Sweet Song of Salvation
Psalm 99 86
That's Why We Sing
Psalm 100 87
Doxology—Thanksgiving
Psalm 101 87
Purity—To Will One Thing!
Psalm 102 88
A Word for the Destitute
Psalm 103 89
My Highest Praise
Psalm 104 91
For the Beauty of the Earth
Psalm 105 92
Blessed Be the Name of the Lord
Psalm 106 94
God of Grace, God of Glory

Book Five: Psalms 107–150

Psalm 107 98
Because of His Love
Psalm 108 100
The Greatness of God's Love
Psalm 109 100
O God, I've Had It with These People
Psalm 110 102
The Lord Provides a Shepherd
Psalm 111 102
Shout to the Lord
Psalm 112 103
A Good Person, Blessed by the Lord
Psalm 113 104
Let the Redeemed Say So
Psalm 114 105
When God Found a Home
Psalm 115 105
It's All About You, Lord
Psalm 116 106
Just Call Me
Psalm 117 107
Praise Him, Praise Him
Psalm 118 107
Unfailing Love
Psalm 119 (176 verses)............109
The A-B-Cs of Faith
Psalm 120 115
A Person of Peace
Psalm 121 115
My Hope Is in You, Lord
Psalm 122 116
Pray for Peace
Psalm 123 116
Keep Your Eyes on the Lord
Psalm 124 117
The Right One on Our Side
Psalm 125 117
What a Mighty God We Serve
Psalm 126 118
Homecoming
Psalm 127 118
The Excitement Is Building
Psalm 128 119
Trust and Obey

Psalm 129 119
A Motherless Child

Psalm 130 120
Out of My Bondage

Psalm 131 120
Pour Contempt on All My Pride

Psalm 132 121
I Love Thy Kingdom, Lord

Psalm 133 122
How Sweet It Is

Psalm 134 122
I Love the Lord

Psalm 135 122
Sing Praises to His Name

Psalm 136 123
A Litany for God's Forever Love

Psalm 137 125
Sweet Homeland

Psalm 138 125
Great Is Thy Faithfulness

Psalm 139 126
The Everlasting Arms

Psalm 140 127
Hear Our Prayer, O Lord

Psalm 141 128
Take Time to Be Holy

Psalm 142 129
Standing in the Need of Prayer

Psalm 143 130
My Faith Looks Up to Thee

Psalm 144 130
A Mighty Fortress

Psalm 145 131
O Worship the King

Psalm 146 133
Our God Reigns

Psalm 147 133
Praise Him, Praise Him

Psalm 148 135
I Stand Amazed

Psalm 149 135
I'll Live for Him

Psalm 150 136
Let All the World in Every Corner Sing

Writer's Note 137

Psalms, Catalogue of Purposes, Suggested Use 139

Foreword

Welcome to the "new psalms"! If you are a regular to devotional reading, you already have a steady diet of inspirational material to keep your spirits challenged. If you are an honest and broad Scripture reader, you know of readings that are less than pleasant or just plain hard to read (and therefore mostly avoided). That goes for personal devotions and congregational reading. Some of them just do not sound nice!

The "old psalms" have these pockets of pedantry, even spewing out occasional curses, "go get 'ems," whines of self-pity, and burn-the-house-down epithets. These we almost never read. Yet we insist on a full reading of all the scriptures to have "real" conversations with God. Here you have them all in today's language, set in today's current flow of life—if you dare read them!

I have been surprised in reading the psalms afresh to find writers so much like me. They pray, plead, cry, whine, and reach glorious heights of poetic utterance. Then they sling mud, demand favors, claim their own righteousness, and even get a bit too big for their britches occasionally.

Mostly I have been surprised by the combative tone and nature of many of the psalms, though the warrior-like posture of such a responsible ruler as David should not surprise me. But right there I have found the most honest picture of my own soul! Real conversations with God, when seen through a mirrored image, can be disarmingly raw, real, and rigorous. It is into that matrix of real conversations that the old psalms have always meant to take us.

Thus, this writer's invitation is to enter into the eternal conversation from old psalms to new with more honesty, fresh language, and eyes wide open. These thoughts are from the scriptures. They just might help you get through!

Bill Henderson

Book One

Psalms 1–41

Psalm 1

God Holds the Secret of True Happiness

(1) Happy is the person who does not follow the advice of fools
or hang around with the wrong crowd
or make friends with cynics.
(2) But this person loves to do what's right
and enjoys the counsel of the scriptures
and takes to heart how to live them,
studying them over and over.
(3) This person flourishes like greenhouse plants,
tended and nourished,
and he or she is fruitful in due time.
They just keep on prospering.
(4) It never happens for those who make a habit
of doing the opposite, refusing counsel and advice.
They are more like dry and crusty plants,
beaten by the weather.
(5) They will never make it to deep satisfaction,
because there will come a time
when they answer for how they lived.
They can't hold up in the company
of people who hold their heads high
and know how to do what is right.
God watches over these.
Ultimately, the way of fools dies with them.

Psalm 2

Proclaiming God's Rule

(1) The nations of the world wield power like they are
in charge of all history,
mocking our God and the people God has given leadership.
(4) The nations conspire while God laughs.
In anger God stumps their plans by
raising up righteous and respected leaders.

(7) God spoke to me. He has chosen me to lead.
He promises all nations under my care.
He pledges strength and courage to lead all these.
(10) Be wise, kings of the nations.
Look to the Lord of all history.
Turn to him in fear and with joy.
(12) Show humility and respect.
He is the God of holy anger and cares for his own.

Psalm 3
Beaten Down, I Shall Rise

(1) My enemies taunt me and say you have no power to help me.
But I know you protect me.
You bless me; you encourage me.
(4) Whenever I cry out, you hear me and never fail to answer.
(5) I sleep restfully like a baby! I do not fear my enemies.
(7) Rise up for me, O God! Save me now!
Deal with those who hurt me as they deserve.
(8) You alone can help and preserve us. Bless your people!

Psalm 4
A Bedtime Prayer

(1) Hear me, Lord! Help me, Lord! Calm me, help me, hear me.
(2) How much longer will fools rule?
How long will they look for love in all the wrong places?
How long will they attack me?
(3) I am trusting God. God is my father who listens when I call.
(4) Watch out! You can go too far! Be humble.
(5) Bring offerings to prove you trust God!
(6) Many question everything good.
Turn on your love light, Lord!
(7) You make me happier than a glass of good wine (or anything on this earth).
(8) Nothing can take away this peace.
You alone take care of me!

Psalm 5

It's a Jungle Out There!

(1) I am praying in desperate hope, as I do every morning.
(4) I know you despise what's wrong.
Haughty people cannot stand up to your peace and power,
for you will crush those who pretend!
(7) I come humbly to church; I am reverent about your people.
(8) Lead me, Lord. Lead me to do what is right;
just make it all clear to me.
(9) Deceitful people harm us all.
Every time they open their mouths, we smell death and destruction.
(10) Come deal with them, Lord! Let them reap what they have sown.
They defy you. Chase them all away!
(11) But we who love you are always joyful.
Protect us as we worship you.
You always turn darkness to light for us. How wonderful!

Psalm 6

Exhausted, I Cry and Pray

(1) I need mercy! I am such a weakling.
How much longer can I hold up?
(4) Your love never fails. I won't be any good as a witness
when I am dead and gone. Use me now!
(6) But I am exhausted from trying to survive.
Tears soak my pillow; I can't stop crying from fear!
(8) Go away, trouble! God is listening for me now!
(9) I cried for mercy, and God heard me.
(10) One day you will regret the trouble you have caused me,
and you will run away in shame!

Psalm 7

I Am at Wit's End!

(1) O Lord God, I run to hide in you.
Help me, and set me free.
My enemy is savage and will devour me like a lion.
(3) But if there is guilt in me, if I have wronged a friend,
or in my pride have stolen from an enemy, turn me over to them.
I don't deserve your help—only justice!
(6) But rise up, O Lord, against unfair enemies.
Demand justice. Bless us, your people!
Judge us all, and see how I have done the best (9) I could.
You alone know what and who are right.
Establish justice, please!
You can do this because you are holy and fair.
If we do not change our ways, you will never let up.
(14) People who do wrong ruin everything around them,
killing our spirits until it all falls in upon themselves.
(17) But I worship you, Lord. I am thankful because you are always so good.

Psalm 8

I Am Amazed at God!

(1) Lord, how glorious you are—always and everywhere!
We can see what you can do by merely looking upward into the skies.
(2) Children love you and need you,
and when they speak, they silence those who doubt you.
(3) Every time I look heavenward
and see the moon and stars in the evening,
I am astonished that you take notice of any of us.
But you made us close to the angels—
beautiful, honorable, and useful.
(6) Everything in this creation is entrusted to us—
beasts, birds, fish, all of it!
You have given it all to us to manage and make useful and keep beautiful.
(9) Lord, how magnificent you are, always and everywhere.

Psalm 9

I Am Gloriously Happy!

(1–2) I am singing, Lord, with all my heart, telling your story.
It makes me happy to sing and shout.
(3) I am stronger because I am joyful,
and people who don't like me stay clear!
You have made me strong.
(5) You control history. Corrupt nations collapse,
and we forget them.
Evil people perish, and their whole civilizations are buried and forgotten.
(7) But, Lord, you reign! You judge! You govern fairly.
You make a home for the homeless and a refuge for us all.
(10) People who have experienced you trust you,
because you have never forgotten
the people who are looking for you.
(16) All of us need to stand up and tell the world your name is *Justice*!
Those who ignore this do so at their own peril.
The poor are always (18) with us, never to be forgotten.
Teach us that precious gift of humility.

Psalm 10

An Evil Man Is Torturing Us! Save Us!

Why, O Lord, do you hide from me?
I am in trouble and cannot find you when I need you!
The wicked ensnares those most vulnerable,
then boasts of his conquests.
Though he curses God, he acts like the master of greed and corruption.
He has no room for God in his proud heart.
(5) But he prospers—bragging, then shaming his opponents.
(6) "I'm top dog. I'm happy. I have no worries!"
(7) His mouth is filthy and deceitful.
(8) He plots ways to overtake the weak
and to capitalize on their misery.
Like a lion, he snares his prey so easily.

Book One: Psalms 1–41

(11) "God pays no attention!" he brags.
(12) O God, don't forget us! Strike back, Lord!
He thinks he has no accountability, but you are watching and waiting.
The weak look to you because you are the helper of orphaned children.
(15) Destroy this cruel man. Show him who is in charge.
(16) The Lord is king forever. All the nations will pay.
(17) Broken people are crying out for you. Encourage them.
(18) Listen, Lord, and defend the weary one,
that this evil man can no longer prevail by harming us.

Psalm 11

It Is Scary Trying to Do Right!

(1) Lord, I hide in you. Don't tell me to run for the hills,
because their weapons can reach us wherever we go.
(3) When the very principles on which we are raised
are ignored and we are overpowered, where can good people go?
But God is in charge! God is on the throne!
He watches us and tests us all.
Testing us, he always hates those who do wrong.
(6) When people arrogantly do what is blatantly wrong,
make no mistake; he will get you in the end!
(7) This is who God is, so holy and pure
that good people seek him always.
God loves fairness!

Psalm 12

It Is Lonely at the Top!

(1) Help me! I feel so alone when I do what is right.
Faithfulness is gone; deceit rules. Sic 'em, Lord!
People brag about being so smart and act like they are gods!
God will rise up because the poor and the weak are crying out to him.
"I will protect them!" God cries, and God never lies.
His words are pure as gold and silver.
(7) I know you will keep us safe and protect us
from the proud,
strutting peacocks who love what is now honored among people—
all that is shameful and disgusting.

Psalm 13

I'm Just Struggling

(1) Have you forgotten me? I can't find you, God.
Is this a game of hide-and-seek?
My thoughts, my conscience, my enemies all torment me.
See me! I am not invisible!
Freshen up my hopes. Do something, or I'll die.
Troubles think they have gotten the best of me. Have they?
But I trust you still love me.
I am full of joy when I remember times you have made a way for me.
(6) I will keep singing, because you have been good to me.

Psalm 14

Where Have All the Good People Gone?

(1) Fools say God doesn't exist.
All the while they revel in living corrupt lives.
Even right (3) under God's watchful eye, they get away with murder.
There is not one single good person left!
(4) Corrupt people never quit. They gobble people up like a tasty dish.
People are terrified, saying, "What's next?" God is with them,

even while greedy people keep taking away all opportunity from them.
I wish churches had an answer.
When God does save these poor people, so beaten down,
the church better stand up and sing and shout!

Psalm 15
Who Is Good Enough to See God?

Lord, who is good enough to stand where you are?
I know—a blameless people, the person who just does what is right.
He or she speaks the truth when nobody else will
and encourages others to do the same.
These people keep their promises even when it makes them unpopular!
(5) No cheating or bribing is possible here.
Those people who persist in doing right cannot be bought.

Psalm 16
So Much to Be Thankful For!

(1) Safety, Lord! I claim you! Without you I am nothing!
(3) The saints have proven this to me. All others fail.
I won't honor them or pretend to worship them.
(5) You are my inheritance, and your boundaries have blessed me.
(7) I have a lot to be thankful for, even all night long.
(8) As I remember you, I grow stronger.
(9) I worship you—in heart and voice and soul.
(10) There is resurrection from the dead awaiting; I know it!
(11) You have taught me how to live and made me happy.
You are always with me, and nothing is finer!

Psalm 17

Troubles Give Way to Trust! I'll See God!

(1) Hear me, Lord; hear me crying from the depth of my heart.
I'm doing the best I know how.
I need you to believe me and tell me so!
(3) Search my heart, Lord, and see I'm trying my best to do right.
Test me, try me, and find me true!
(4) I am steering clear of those untrustworthy ones, just as you said.
I follow in your ways alone, never veering off your path.
(6) Now I call you because I know you always answer; please hear me.
(7) Your love is wonderful, reaching out so lovingly to all who run to you.
Show us that again.
Show how you have chosen me and tenderly care for me. Shelter me.
(9) People laugh at me and hate me for trying to do right.
Show them you love me.
They are wickedly proud, like lions hunting for their prey.
(10) They have shut you out, bragging about their exploits,
and they watch me like an enemy.
Rise up! Get in their faces.
Prove your power is over me.
(13) You never fail to feed the hunger of those who yearn for you,
those who love you.
The generations of faithful people keep getting the help they need,
prospering, getting stronger and stronger.
(15) That's why I know you will one day bring me home;
I know I'll meet you one day!
I'll wake up from my death,
and I'll see you face to face! Hooray!

Psalm 18

God Is Faithful and Beautiful!

(1) I love you, Lord of my strength!
The Lord is my anchor, my sanctuary, and my safety!
God is so strong, and I run to the Lord for help.

God is a never-ending resource. God is due all of my praise.
God has never failed me or anyone.
(4) I faced death, and God was there.
It was so real that I felt like I was dying. But I called on the Lord.
I cried like I was drowning, hanging on for the last time, sobbing in church,
and that's where the Lord heard me and answered.
(7) When God answered, it seemed the whole earth shook in terror
at God's anger for my troubles.
Heaven broke open. Thunder and lightning flashed.
Angels flew everywhere and brought the Lord right to me in the wind.
Then, suddenly, it was night, and God hid. Then again, the sun burst forth,
and the thunder and lightning kept right on, stronger than ever.
(16) Even the seas roared, but God was there for me. I felt his love.
It was disastrous everywhere I tried to go,
but God held on and saved me just because he loved me.
(20) God saved me because I am always trying to do right.
I have never tucked in my tail and run from my God,
and now I believe God is rewarding me.
(25–26) God, you are faithful to faithful people, pure to those who are pure.
But when we do wrong, we see just how hard you can be.
(27) God, you reach for those who are humble
and let the proud just hang themselves.
Give me oil for my lamp; keep me burning!
God, you are amazing—turning my darkness to brightness,
my weakness to strength, all my impossibilities to possibilities!
I can run up a wall!
Let's face it, (30) God's ways are perfect. God's word is perfect. God is for us!
(31) God is number one. God makes me capable to climb,
nimble to hike, strong for battle, set for greatness!
(38–42) All my enemies crumble when God is with me.
(43) You set me up as a leader, even of people I was unaware of.
(44–45) Strangers obey me and bow before me.
(46) God is alive! Praise to my rock! God is for me!
(49) I'll tell the world! Nobody can touch God's greatness.
(50) All the leaders of the world who serve the Lord
will always be winners and always feel God smiling on them.

Psalm 19

Living Words Are Everywhere

(1) All the heavens shout out about our glorious God,
and the skies show what God can do!
Every day, we hear God speaking; every night, we learn more.
Everywhere we hear and learn, God is behind it all,
and it goes out to all the world. Creation is God's best testimony!
(4) Look at the sun. God put it in place so perfectly and beautifully.
It looks like a proud groom stepping into his wedding
or like an Olympic champion happily running his race.
The whole world is subject to its warmth.
(7) God's teachings are perfect, bringing life to your bones.
God's principles for living give life to dying dreams.
God's word is right on target every time.
(9) When we respect God, our hearts are pure forever,
because what God asks for is all wonderfully pure.
(10) And that's better than anything money can buy!
God can keep us free of stupid mistakes.
(12) We are all selfishly wrong at times and need God's mercy.
(14) Lord, thanks for letting me get things off my chest.
Thanks for listening. I want only to please you with my ramblings,
because you are so good to me.

Psalm 20

A Prayer for My Friends

(1) I pray that the Lord will always listen to you when you are troubled,
always protect you when you are alone.
God will help us all with help from God's church.
May God remember how you have been so faithful.
(4) May God bless your hopes and dreams and help you succeed in everything.
We'll be right behind you as you win the day,
praising God all the way as your prayers are answered.
(6) I am convinced he watches those whom he puts in places of leadership,
answering with power to do right.

(7) Some people feel like being wealthy and successful
is the way to make it in life, but trusting God is the only way to go.
We rise up tall while the others just shrink up and fall.
(9) O Lord, give us your chosen and blessed leaders!
Answer our prayers!

Psalm 21

Our God Is a Winner!

(1) Lord, you are a winner, and your leaders know it.
They are blessed.
Their prayers are answered, every single one.
You alone started this when you blessed them, body and soul,
as you always do.
Everybody sees how great you are when our leaders succeed.
They are so obviously surrounded by your presence
and made to be so happy.
Surely this is forever!
When a leader completely trusts you, they can never fail!
(8) Not so with the proud God-deniers.
You have got them by the throat.
When you are ready and the time is right,
you will snuff them out like a burned-out candle.
Even their whole family line will disappear.
(11) No matter how hard they try,
when they deny you, they are bound to fail.
They will run for the hills of obscurity when you take them on.
(13) O Lord, you are magnificent!

Psalm 22

Despair!

(1) O God, you have forgotten me. Why do you ignore me?
I never quit crying out for you. The church has never stopped praising you.
Our families have always trusted you, and you have never failed them!
But I am worthless and hopeless.
(8) Everybody laughs at me, saying, "He talks about God! Let God save him!"
Lord, you birthed me from my mother,
teaching me to trust you even from my mother's breast.
Now I need you most; don't forget me!
(12) It seems the powerful are out to shame me.
The cruelest power-mongers discredit me, and I am worn out!
Even the knit-pickers are tearing me up! I am sick as a dog—physically sick!
(18) Now I am losing everything I own.
(19) Don't hide from me. You have always been my strength.
Help now—as always!
(22) I'll praise you; I'll tell the world!
(23) Let the church stand up and shout and be counted:
"God never forgets us! He answers all our prayers!"
(25) You inspire me when I stand up to speak.
I will keep giving my tithes and offerings.
(26) Nobody in need who seeks you will go hungry, Lord!
One day the whole world will know and see you, Lord!
Every family on earth will bow before you one day,
(28) because you truly are the Lord of all!
(29) The rich and the poor will sing the same praises.
Even future generations will hear and trust you
and proclaim the same songs of testimony to your faithfulness.
You never fail. We will tell them all!

Psalm 23

His Shepherding Love

(1) The Lord is my shepherd! He gives me everything I need.
(2) He gives me rest when I need it,
and he takes me to refreshing waters.
(3) He can calm me and renew me when I most need it.
He shows me what is right, how to stand up for him.
(4) I have been in deep trouble before, next to death even,
yet I have learned never to be afraid,
because I can feel your presence always.
You have everything, all the tools necessary to keep me from falling and failing.
(5) It is a feast to belong to you,
especially when my enemies come after my neck.
You heal my injuries. I am amazed.
(6) I guess this is your plan and your way—to be so powerful
and full of love for those who look to you.
I'll never leave you, Lord!

Psalm 24

The Lord, Strong and Mighty!

(1) This world belongs to God; all the creatures,
all the creation, all the people are God's.
God has brought life out of the seas and built it up on the oceans.
(3) Knowing the Lord is so mighty, who among us can stand before him in
his presence?
Any person who simply tries to do what is right, whose motives are pure.
Anybody who does not pretend that anything is greater than God
or who pretends to do right.
(5) That person can stand before God and will be blessed.
These are people who are yours, O Lord!
(7) Swing wide open the church doors within which God is welcomed.
Who is this God? The powerful and mighty Lord,
the one who whips all the pretenders.
So open up! Welcome God inside!

(10) Who is this God again?
It's the God we all know is so magnificent!
Let him in!

Psalm 25

Forgive Me, Lord

(1) I turn to you, Lord. I'm trusting you.
Don't let me be made a fool, otherwise, my enemies win out!
(3) Nobody who trusts you will ever be shamed,
but people who intentionally do wrong will never make it!
(4) Let me see what's right. Teach me, Lord.
Show me the truth as only you can, Lord.
(6) Come forth with forgiveness as you have done for centuries.
I have been a fool growing up, and I need your forgiveness.
(8) God is Good.
God teaches what's right to those who are wrong.
God loves everybody who tries to do what is right.
That's why I ask for forgiveness.
(12) Where are those who seek God?
He'll teach you so you can get your feet on the right path
and your family will be blessed.
(14) He will tell you his secrets and whisper his love to you.
I am seeking the Lord, for he is my only hope.
(16) Look at me, Lord, because I am so weak; I am alone and weary.
The harder I try, the worse it gets, it seems.
Look at me, Lord, and forgive me.
(19) Bad guys seem to be winning; they hate me,
but don't let them.
All I have is my integrity.
Save me, because I trust only in you.
(22) Save all your people, O Lord,
from everything that makes us stumble!

Psalm 26

Test Me—Try Me

(1) Prove me rightly, Lord.
I have never consciously brought shame to your name.
(2) Test me, try me, examine my heart and my mind,
because I keep your promises before me always.
(4) I choose my friends carefully,
and I don't put up with two-faced people.
I hate the gatherings of snide and scoffing people.
(6) I run to church sometimes just to feel like I am clean again!
And I do when I tell about the things I have seen you do!
(8) I love my church, the place where we can learn of you.
(9) Please don't ever take that excitement away from me.
Please don't think I am with those scoffers and doubters.
They are relentless in their schemes to get ahead.
(11) I may be slow, but my heart is pure.
And whenever I am with your people, my heart is full of joyful praise.
Have mercy on me, Lord.

Psalm 27

God Never Fails

(1) God is joy and freedom for me. Why would I ever be afraid?
God is a place for me to be safe. Who can scare me now?
(2) Whenever powerful people rise up and do wrong,
whenever people taunt me for trying to do what's right,
they will always, ultimately, trip over their own egos.
(3) If a whole nation of wrong attacked me, I would never be afraid;
I'd rise up.
(4) I only ask one thing of my God, one thing I will pursue—
that I always have a church, a place to see God and learn of his strength.
He will always be there for me, especially when I am depressed.
(6) I'll be the one shouting his praises,
because I will feel secure with him. Just listen to my songs!
(7) Please listen to me, Lord. Answer when I call.

My heart prompts me even if my own family should misunderstand me, Lord.
I know you will always accept me.
Show me the path, and I'll walk in it! Don't let me be misled.
I am sure that I will see your hands where people love you.
(14) Be patient, my heart. Be strong, be courageous, and be patient!

Psalm 28

Calling on the Lord

(1) I call on you, Lord. Don't ignore me. If you do, I'm as good as dead.
(3) Two-faced people love to play the game of
pretending to be your people,
but they will surely reap what they sow. Let 'em have it!
(5) They just ignore you, God; don't let 'em get away with it.
You will show them, Lord!
(6) God is great; God is good. He has heard me crying.
The Lord alone is my strength and my protection.
I am exploding with confident joy and thanks.
(8) The Lord is always the strength of his people, a virtual fortress for us all.
(9) Save us and bless us, because we are yours.
Be like a shepherd with sheep. Lift us; carry us forever.

Psalm 29

Worship Like It's Supposed to Be

(1) Announce that the Lord is glorious!
Say that he is strong,
you who are the strongest and mightiest among us all.
(3) He speaks and controls the waters.
God thunders over the mighty seas, and his will is powerful.
(5) When God's voice roars, the great trees shake and shatter.
That's God's will you hear in the thunder and lightning.
(6) As God roars, God makes the faithful lands skip and jump like calves
and young bulls.
Even the desert sands blow when God speaks.
God can disturb the calmest places we know.

When God speaks mightily to us all,
we should gather in church and recognize his power and shout "Glory!"
(10) God is king and ruler over the seas and will never falter.
(11) God will give his people all the strength they need.
That is God's blessing of peace to us.

Psalm 30
Why We Praise Him

(1) I will praise you, Lord, because you pulled me up from depression;
you saved me from ridicule.
When I called, you answered and healed.
I thought I was almost dead, but you wouldn't have it.
(4) All of us should be singing praises.
We've experienced God's heavy hand, but it only lasts a moment.
The worst trouble only lasts overnight until he lifts us up again.
(6) I boasted proudly when you made me strong.
You had put my feet on solid ground,
but then you hid from me, and I realized I was acting haughty.
I cried out.
I begged, knowing that I couldn't be a witness
to your glorious goodness and grace if I was dead.
I pled, "Hear me, Lord! Help me! Be forgiving!"
(11) Before I knew it, I was dancing for joy again;
(12) you want us to be praising and singing and not to be mum!
That's why I'll never stop thanking you, Lord!

Psalm 31
Words for Worship

(1) I have come to you for strength. Never let me fall.
You are holy, pure love, and I welcome your leading spirit
and your guidance over me.
(4) I am such a doomed and selfish person.
Set me free from such a trap.
I give you my heart and soul. Make me useful again, Lord.

(6) I watch people put their trust in their wealth, possessions, and power,
and I know how foolish that is.
I place my trust in you alone. I am overshadowed by your mighty love.
You saw me when I was at my worst, and your love never let me go.
(9) I feel so weak, Lord.
My eyes, my body, my heart, my strength fail me.
Sometimes I feel like the laughingstock of the whole town,
like people wish I were dead.
(14) But I tell them that you alone are worthy.
All my days are in your hands.
Prove your love and strength through my life.
Prove your holiness and power by shaming our contemptible bad-mouthers.
(19) Your greatness is wonderful,
and we who follow you find refuge in you.
(22) Praise the Lord, for he has blessed us.
I cried out, and God heard me.
(23) Love the Lord, openly and joyfully,
because he gives us full and abundant life,
but he cuts down the prideful at the knees.
(24) This is our hope and strength.
Have courage, all you people who trust God!

Psalm 32

All About Forgiveness

(1–2) Oh how clean the feeling, to know when God forgives you,
to know our foolish ways can be amended.
How happy we can be when we decide to come clean.
(3) When I held my secrets within, I was dying inside.
I felt your disappointment like summer's hot, burning sun.
(5) So I encourage everyone who trusts God to pray when close to the Lord,
because when troubles consume us, it is harder to be honest.
But I have found how true you are. You give me a song!
(7) You teach me; you guide my steps; you advise my thoughts.
Don't be stubborn as a mule.
Horses, too, have to be ridden with a bit in their mouths.

When we buck you, Lord, our troubles only increase,
when love could be our better choice.
Be happy, good people. Sing joyfully all you who choose the love of God.

Psalm 33
God Has Plans

(1) Sing joyfully! It looks good on you!
Use every musical instrument and every new tune
to show your happiness in God.
(5) God is always faithful and true.
He loves us when we do right and when we act fairly to others.
The evidence is in every corner of the world.
(6) When God spoke, the heavens and the stars were formed;
he contained the sea.
(8) Everyone all over the world knows that and respects God.
(9) God merely spoke, and all creation began.
God rules the nations, confusing people's best plans.
(11) But God's plans never change and never fail;
nor do the people God chooses to demonstrate his love.
(13) God sees us from heaven because he made us.
War never saved anybody, ultimately,
no matter how great our armies.
God is watching those who call out to him,
delivering them and providing.
(20) We pray to you, Lord. You make us glad.
We wait for you. You alone are our help and hope.

Psalm 34
Praise, Praise, and Practice!

(1) I will praise God always. (3) Won't you join with me?
When I call, he answers.
Anyone who calls to him shines! I did.
There are angels all around, working God's powerful love.
(8) Try it; you'll like him. You will be blessed.

Show God respect, and see how God provides.
(10) Even mighty lions have to keep hunting to live.
For us, a thimble full of faith is enough for a lifetime.
(11) Children, come to me, and I will teach you how.
If you want the best in life, be honest! Do right!
Find what makes for peace and work at it.
God will never overlook a life like this,
and he listens attentively.
He ignores people who choose a wrong path,
and ultimately they are forgotten.
(17) But good, humble people call to God,
and he hears, and he delivers,
especially people who live with disappointment.
(19) Don't get me wrong;
good people aren't immune to life's troubles,
yet God never turns his back on us.
(20) Some testify that not a hair on their heads
has been harmed.
(21) Choose wrong and it will eat you alive!
Choose wrong and you wear a brand—"I'm doomed!"
(22) But try constantly to do right,
and God will always make it good!

Psalm 35

Battling with God as My Helper

(1) Put on your armor, God! We've got enemies.
Remind me of your promised love and care.
(4) Cursed be my enemies! Shame on you!
You are lightweight boxers against God's heavyweight angels.
You're on a dark escape route, while the angels of God are in hot pursuit!
(7) Because of your sneaky ways, my God surprises you!
(9) I'll be cackling when I see you fall.
(10) I'll be amazed in the presence of my warrior-like God.
(11) It has been a big eye-opener to try to befriend my so-called friends.
They have stabbed me in the back when I had gone to bat for them.

(17) Lord, how long will you put up with this?
Help me, and I will sing out among the crowds.
(19) Don't let this go on any longer.
They are only pretending to be at peace while they fatten their nests.
(22) I know you have seen it. Come now, and put a stop to it!
(25) They think they are gaining ground. For shame!
(27) Let my true friends see the truth and be joyfully proclaiming your power!
(28) I, for one, will never be silent about my wonderful God!

Psalm 36
A Message to This World

(1) I have a message about this world.
It comes from deep within, from my heart.
People have lost their fear of God! People are so full of their own pride
that they cannot see the forest for the trees, their own foolishness.
They have lost their common sense, and they don't know it.
They don't do what's right anymore.
(4) They lie awake at night and dream of ways to become greater and greater.
They cannot see how destructive their chosen path is.
(5) How different is the Lord! The greatest love ever, the truest heart ever,
the purest path ever, kindness and fairness ever!
The lessons are all over your creation.
You made a good life for both people and animals.
Your love is worth any sacrifice we could ever make.
The rich and the poor alike find your goodness and grace.
It's a feast to belong to you. It's a thrilling pleasure.
You have all we need to live wisely.
Don't let up, Lord. You are good to us when we are good.
Reassure me of your protective hands.
Look how the wrong stumble into oblivion!

Psalm 37

Never, Never, Never Quit!

(1) Never grow weary because of those who prosper while doing wrong.
They'll get theirs one day.
It will only last a fleeting moment, as they will wither like day plants.
Don't worry.
(3) Trust in the Lord. Do what is right. Bloom where you are planted.
Take delight in the Lord, and he will fulfill your dreams.
Make promises to God and keep them. He never fails.
He will use your good life to be a blessing,
like a lighthouse for struggling sailors in this world.
When you decide to live right, God will bless others through your life.
(7) But you must be patient before God.
Don't lose it
when the hotshots act like they have the upper hand.
(8) Don't lose your cool. Take a deep breath. Two wrongs don't make a right.
(9) Wrong never, never succeeds in the end. Good people do.
(10) Give it time. The bad guys disappear one by one.
(11) Humility leads to peace and eventually wins it all.
(12) Though meanness is scary, the Lord laughs at them.
(14) Though meanness looks so strong
and steps on the little people to get ahead,
in the end they only hurt themselves.
(16) God is on the side of humble servants.
Humble lives are better than all the accolades of the hotshots.
(18) God knows your days—they are in his hands.
You are stronger than you think.
(20) Wickedness perishes. Wickedness cheats us all.
Good people can't stop giving to help others.
(23) When God knows you are trying, he makes you able.
You might stumble, but you will never fall. God's got you!
(25) As I have grown old and look back, I realize I have never seen
God's people abandoned—generation after generation.
Decide now to live good lives,
because you will feel God's love, faithfulness, and protection.

(30) You will become wise, a fine statesman for good.
You will know what is good, because it is deep inside you.
No matter who rises up against you, they will fail.
(34) Be patient before the Lord. Just wait and see.
(35) I have seen the mighty look so great but soon fall.
They were soon nowhere to be found.
(37) Watch those people you know who live right.
See how they find peace. Not like the bad guys.
(39) And that's exactly what God planned.
God is making plans now, and your best days are ahead!

Psalm 38

Sometimes I Goof Up, God

(1) God, have mercy. I'm really losing it here.
I feel guilty, sick, and depressed.
(5) I'm not sure I can make it this time.
Nobody to blame but myself. I'm hurting inside and out.
(9) But you know that, since you know everything.
And all my friends and neighbors see me slipping
and wonder if I'm losing it.
(13) I am deaf and dumb, unable to respond.
I wait for you, Lord, and you always answer.
(17) I screwed up, big time, and I am paying a high price.
I have given all my enemies plenty of ammunition,
and they're gunning for me. Stupid me!
(21) Don't turn your back on me, God.
Come. Come quickly. I always call you "my savior."

Psalm 39

I Want Out!

(1) I committed myself to live a more careful and proper life,
but deep inside it was killing me.
It burned me up when people seemed to get away with murder!
So I spoke up, finally.
(4) Lord, show me when this unfair trip is over. Life is not fair. I want out.
Life is just like a gasp for breath. We all try to survive,
and sometimes we make it good, only to have nobody to pass it on to.
(7) So what do I have to look forward to?
I have always lived for you, always counted on you. Don't let me down.
I accept your discipline, but enough is enough.
You discipline us all when we get too big for our britches.
Hear me, Lord, because I feel so far from you.
(13) Stop bearing down on me, Lord,
so I can have a little joy in my life!
Stop it, or I am going to quit!

Psalm 40

Swallowed Up in Troubles

(1) When I was patient before the Lord, he heard me.
He caught me just in time.
He pulled me out of the filth of life and helped me find all that is good again.
(3) God set my heart singing again and taught me how to praise him!
Because of my music, many others will turn to the
Lord and give him their lives.
(4) God can use any one of us
if we turn to him and are true and do not chase false gods.
(5) You have done so much, Lord. Your plans keep coming.
If I tried to count my blessings,
I would be overwhelmed.
(6) I tried to please you with my offerings, but all you wanted was my heart.
I kept heaping it on until I finally said, "I want to follow you, Lord,"
and I meant it from my heart.

Book One: Psalms 1–41

(9) I stand and tell everyone at church.
I just can't shut up about it. I keep telling them all.
(11) Let your mercy surround and cover me fully
instead of these troubles that surround me.
I'm weak as water. (13) Help, Lord. Quick! Please!
Confound and disgrace those who (16) try to put me down.
Let us rejoice while these idiots are brought to shame.
God is good—praise him! I am so weak and so in need of you. Help me!

Psalm 41

The Great Physician

(1) God bless us when we tend to be weak.
God bless us and make us his own possession.
I know God will help you when you are sick and bring you back to health.
(4) I have asked God to heal me. I have done wrong,
and I am paying the price for my ways. I am sick.
(5) Enemies think I am dying. The people who visit me are horrified.
They hate to look at me. They would rather I just die.
"He'll never make it!" they say.
(9) My best friend has joined these doubters.
(10) Lord, you won't let me down, I am sure. Raise me up.
I want to prove these so-called friends wrong.
(18) I have served you well and kept doubters at bay. That's living proof.
You always held me up and drew me close,
because I am trying my best to be true.
(13) God is great; God is good, the God of his people.
He is always and eternally the same. Amen.

Book Two

Psalms 42–72

Psalm 42

There Is a Hunger Within

(1) Just as a deer pants for the streams of water,
so do I thirst for you, O God.
(2) Deep inside, I crave the refreshment I find in you
because you are alive, fresh, and fulfilling.
(3) I am tired of this tearful sadness, day and night,
while I am taunted by people who ask,
"Why doesn't your God come around when you are down?"
(4) These things encourage me as I reflect: the joyful walks
with the crowds into church, shouting, singing, thanking, and praising you.
(5) So why do I get so blue? Trust this joyful God again!
You know you will always get up when you are down!
When I am down, I will remember these mountaintop experiences.
(7) I am stirred deep within when I see and hear the roaring waterfalls.
Ocean waves remind me!
(8) In the daytime I feel your love; at night the melody lingers always
as a prayer in my heart to the God of my every day.
(9) I speak to God, who anchors me, saying,
"Have you forgotten me and turned toward my enemy instead?"
They are taunting me when I drag around like an abandoned puppy.
I feel lost deep inside at times.
"Where is your big bad God now?"
(11) "Don't be dragging around," I say within. "Why give up like this?
God is faithful—hope in him."
I am going to praise him yet! I know it! God is my savior!

Psalm 43

Send the Light

(1) Prove me right, O Lord. I stand up against it all when my nation turns vile and immoral.
(2) I need to feel the strength I know you have.
You haven't forgotten, have you?
Then why am I looking like a downhearted fool?
(3) "Send the light—the blessed gospel light. Let it shine from shore to shore."
Let it show me the path again to your strong presence.
(4) When I am led to it, I will write up a new hymn and melody
that everyone will love.
(5) Stop this whining! "Screw your courage to the sticking place!"
I know I will praise you once more. My God is my savior!

Psalm 44

You're in Charge, Though Sometimes It's Hard!

(1) We have heard the witness of our family ancestors who trusted you.
You gave them land and drove out their enemies. You made them prosper.
Enough said!
(3) Their armies didn't do it. It was you alone, O Lord,
because they were not afraid to trust in your providential love.
(4) You are the king of glory!
You made a nation for yourself,
and we win only through your will and power.
I won't rely on my power but on your power. You did it.
(9) But it seems different now.
You allowed us to lose and to be defeated.
You turned us completely over to them.
(12) It is just as if you threw us away
and allowed us to be the joke of the town.
Others have heard, and they have pity on us;
how our fortunes have turned.
(15) I just want to hide my face in shame.
Those who always disagreed with me want to cash in on it now!

(17) What happened? Did I miss something?
We have been faithfully following you
and the covenant we made together.
(18) We have been true inwardly in our hearts
as well as keeping our witness pure.
But you didn't see that and have now let us be put to shame.
(20) We could understand it if we deserved a thrashing for our behavior
or ran after false gods.
You would know because you know everything.
We have even faced death for the sake of your truth,
like sheep led to slaughter.
(23) Wake up, Lord.
Where have you gone?
You are overlooking this misery of your own children.

Psalm 45

A Wedding Song

(1) I am inspired by this high moment of our king's life.
I want to honor him with this poem.
(2) You are an exceptional person,
and you speak with God's graceful blessings.
(3) Put on your armor; be clothed in your great honor,
and ride out like the winner you are,
because you represent truth, humility, and goodness.
Show your stuff; you have earned it.
(5) Rise up against foolish rulers, and let their nations see your winning side.
Your rule commands attention
because you stand for justice and fair treatment for all,
and because you will not stand for wrong to go unaddressed.
That's why God has set you up as the leader,
giving you a joyful spirit.
(8) Even your outfits inspire us with ancient fragrances.
You come from great places where the music is glorious.
You have drawn the attention of the daughters of rulers of all nations,
and now you have chosen the most beautiful to be your bride.

(10) Listen, lovely bride; don't be afraid to leave your own homeland.
The king idolizes you. You can respect him,
because he is thoroughly honorable and trustworthy.
(12) You'll see, especially when the other great people of the world
come to honor you and gift you.
(13) You are so beautiful! Look at you in your own suite and your regal robes!
You process to the king, all your bridesmaids following,
singing, dancing, clapping!
(16) Your children will soon become your home place,
and your love will make them good for the people.
(17) I will remember this day as long as I live and beyond!
You will be remembered by the whole world!

Psalm 46

Never Fear; God Is Here

(1) God is so great that all of us can find safety and comfort.
Let the whole world crumble, but we won't fear anything.
Let the mountains tumble into the sea as its roaring
and surging waves eat them up.
(4) There is a calm river flowing into the place where God's people are,
and it will supply our every need.
(5) God is there, and that makes everything okay.
God always helps us right in the nick of time.
(6) The world's nations are the same. They rise up; then they implode.
God speaks, and this world brings fear and life.
(7) God is here, right here with us, a strong fortress.
Come see and be amazed. He brings peace; sometimes it comes hard.
(10) Quietly rest, and you can experience how God does it.
The nations are coming around to his greatness.
(11) God almighty is here. God is strong.

Psalm 47

God Is Great; God Is Good!

(1) Praise him, every nation! Shout about it,
and be joyful to our awesome God. God is the king over the earth.
(3) God hands the nations over to us.
He hand-picks our inheritance, because he loves us that much!
(5) God's presence rises as we sing and shout and make music.
(6) Sing with us! Sing to the Lord. He is the king of everything,
so sing in joyful song!
He rules, reigns, and judges the nations as we all gather before him,
knowing we belong to him.
(7) How great is the Lord!

Psalm 48

Great God! Check Him Out at Church!

(1) God is greater than our minds can comprehend.
The only way to approach God properly is with praise!
(2) Come see how we praise him in his house.
It is wonderful and joyful, like the highest mountaintop.
God is present there always, protecting and watching.
(4) How silly are the rulers of pagan nations.
When they see his wonders, they run like scalded dogs, howling in pain,
like a woman screaming in labor pains.
(7) And God crushes them like toothpicks,
like the tiny boats smashed against the mighty sea winds.
God does just what he said he would do; he stands strong for us.
(9) We come to church to be reminded of this: that your love never fails
and your praise can be heard worldwide.
(10) Your character is known, seen, and heard, like your praise, worldwide.
(11) Everyone you touch turns toward what is good!
Your church rejoices. People of God are glad because you are fair to us all.
(12) I challenge you, people. Go to any strong church and count her
missions in action, the people she reaches toward and helps.
Just see her strength shared worldwide! Tell it to your children.

(14) What you see is what you will always get with God.
Our God is the same every day, guiding right on through eternity.

Psalm 49
It's God, Not Your Money, You Fool!

(1) Listen up, everyone. I am calling everyone, rich and poor, low and high.
I am about to bring you a song.
I believe God's spirit has inspired a poem right from my heart,
a puzzle for you to grasp.
(5) Why would I ever be afraid in troubling times,
surrounded by the worst of humanity, big, rich, powerful fat-cats?
(7) No one can beat back death, which one day will stalk and conquer us all;
no one can pay off God and beat death.
The cost would be enormous and impossible.
(9) No one can live forever!
(10) Everybody knows the good ones, the smart ones, and the rich ones
die just like the bad ones, the foolish, the poor.
"You can't take it with you," they say. Nothing goes into our graves.
(12) No matter how much we accumulate,
we still do not or cannot avoid the final end of life.
We are no different from the animals in that regard.
(13) Especially those who only have themselves to thank for all they have.
Even worse, they are like sheep—when they die, nobody cares! But the
people who love God keep trusting him while the others just rot away!
(15) Yet God has a plan for me. The grave is not the final word.
I'm going to live with God!
(16) So do not be impressed with a person's riches or their house size,
for it stays when he or she goes.
Nobody will ask in heaven, "How big was your house?"
(19) Though she assumed prominence and praise for being prosperous,
she'll die just like all of us,
especially like her own kind who will never see eternity.
(20) A person who is rich but thinks he got it all by himself
and doesn't acknowledge God's hand in his blessings
still dies just like the animals.

Psalm 50

Looking for a Thankful Heart

(1) God speaks! A mighty one with a mighty voice,
from sunup to sundown, calling the earth to life.
(2) From God's house, so beautiful, God is shining out like a lighthouse.
(3) Our God comes forth and speaks out loud!
Lightning and storms pave the way as he calls out to heaven and earth
to gather up for judging his people.
"Gather them up, these my people," he calls.
"They made a covenant promise with sacrifices!"
(6) And the heavens proclaim his perfect holiness as the judge of us all!
Then God speaks: (7) "Listen up, my people;
I have a bone to pick with you all, because I alone am God.
(8) This is not about your offerings.
You can't begin to give me enough, because I own it all,
all the living creatures! Mine!
(12) If I had an appetite like you do,
you would be the last place I would turn. It's all mine anyway.
Do I need your offerings? Not really, but it serves as a
good discipline for you. So keep it up,
and keep calling on me when you get to the end of your rope.
I will answer, as I always have. You can count on me.
(16) Not so for the hypocrites who quote my words
but do not bother to ever understand and follow them.
Why you bother, I do not know!
You have made better connections with greedy thieves than with me.
You are now mouthing their arrogant claims like you are one of them,
instead of one of your better kind. (21) I waited for you,
thinking you would see the light. But now I look you in the eye.
(22) It is high time for you to pay attention to me,
or you will die like an enemy of mine.
(23) It is a thankful heart I am looking for. Gratitude.
That is proof of your faithfulness.
That honors me.
That opens the doors of hearts everywhere.

That makes it possible for me to show the power
I have been planning to freely give to help you."

Psalm 51
Mercy Trumps Punishment

(1) Today, I need mercy from your heart of love.
Only your mercy can clean up my mess and
wash the filth away. Clean up my sin.
(3) I know my wrongs. They haunt me,
and I know they represent my hidden need to be God!
You are justified when you call me out. I deserve it.
I have been sinful since the day I was born. It is in my DNA.
(6) But I know what you want within my heart—honesty.
I feel you urging me all the time.
(7) I guess a good whipping is all that has ever worked with me.
If you will apply the belt,
I will become clean as snow again.
Shame on me!
(8) I want to sing out joyfully again,
like an honest follower.
(9) Look away from my foolish ways.
See how hard I am trying in my heart.
Cleanse my heart, O God!
Make me a sturdy and resolute follower again.
(11) In my shame I need you more than ever.
I need your Spirit.
I need that joy down inside.
I need a real commitment again.
(13) I'll have a story to tell to the nations
that will turn their hearts to the light!
But now my shame threatens to ruin my witness.
(15) O Lord, let me live in praise and singing.
I know my offerings alone cannot make me right again.
You want that humility, not that chip on my shoulder.
You have never turned your back on genuine humility.

(18) Make your church blossom and flourish.
We need new strength in our old ways.
(19) When you make our hearts pure,
then our offerings will be genuine again.
Then our offerings will be adequate to cover every need.

Psalm 52

The Young and the Restless

(1) You braggart! What do you get out of being so proud and mouthy?
You're fooling nobody—and (2) certainly not God.
You think you can have it both ways, talking out of all sides of your mouth.
Your tongue is hurtful, deceiving, and just plain dirty.
I am afraid to be around you,
because God will not turn a blind eye to your cruelty.
You're gonna really catch it!
(6) The people who try to do right all have your number.
 "There he goes again!
He thinks his wealth will buy him security rather than God.
He got where he is by stepping on the little people, the weak and helpless."
(5) But I have deep roots in God, and that has paid off.
I am like the magnificent plants throughout the church.
It is all because I have built my life trusting in God's grace.
(9) Let me praise you, Lord, for all you have done.
I trust you, and I proudly bear your name—it is beautiful and good!
Let me stand up and be counted among all your faithful people.

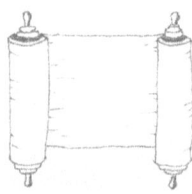

Psalm 53
Yes, God Is Still There!

(1) I heard a fool say to himself, "There is no God!"
But his life was pure trash, falling apart, worthless!
(2) God is watching us, searching for any who really get it,
any who really want to know God.
Regrettably, not one single person wants to get the real thing.
We have lost our desire to do what is right.
(4) When will we ever learn?
There is a generation who thoughtlessly gobbles up the good, simple people.
But why have we lost our nerve?
A closer look will prove that God is faithful,
that God is punishing the shameful people right along.
They aren't getting away with all that they think—
or that we think, for that matter.
(6) I wish greater help and greater hope for God's people
were coming from our churches.
When God finally decides to come through for us,
"We will sing and shout the victory!"

Psalm 54
Enemies on My Left, God on My Right!

(1) Save me, O Lord! I am going down for the final time.
You are known for your strength, and I need you now.
Are you listening? Can you hear me now?
(3) It's those troublemakers again,
and this time they want to completely snuff me out, along with my witness.
(4) I believe you can help me, Lord, because you always have.
Be faithful now, and let their slander fall back on them.
(6) I keep right on tithing. I keep right on praising.
And it still feels good!
You have never let me down;
I've watched you overcome wrong over and over and over!

Psalm 55

A Single Plea for Help

(1) Here I come on my bended knees again.
Lord, I need you. Listen and answer as you promised.
It's my own thinking that is driving me crazy.
I hear my opponents; I see the glaring eyes;
I feel their veiled threats and the heart of their angry contempt.
(4) I can hardly stand it. I feel like I've about had it.
Never have I felt like such a pitiful baby—scared, terrified, outnumbered.
(6) I have been telling my friends, "If I had wings, I would flee this place.
I'd go to a deserted place, seeking shelter from all this agonizing heartache."
(9) Lord, deal with these arrogant and prideful fools.
Make them sound like the idiots they are, because they are ruining our city.
They complain constantly. Nothing about our home is good enough for them,
and they stir up trouble everywhere they go.
(12) If it were just one troublemaker calling me names, I could handle it.
If I had one real enemy out to get me, I would just go someplace else.
(13) But this is my friend, one I once trusted like a brother,
one I shared my church leadership with.
(15) I hope an early death overtakes them all!
It's getting worse by the day, and it has to stop!
(16) Nevertheless, I call to God, and he gives me strength
morning, noon, and night. Every time I pray, God answers.
(18) Not a hair on my head is harmed, regardless how big my battle.
It's God's world, God's throne, God's way
with people who insist on doing wrong.
(20) I have heard my dear friend ignore his promise to God.
His talk is smooth, but his heart is twisted. His words are fighting words.
Here's the promise—throw your burden on God,
and he will give you strength to conquer it. He always does that.
God will deal with those who do wrong. But I choose to trust him forever.

Psalm 56
Another Plea for Help

(1) It's your mercy that will sustain me.
The idiots still attack when I stand up for you.
Whenever I am afraid, I turn to you. What have I to fear?
(5) They misquote me; they plot to undo what I have done; they never let up.
(7) Don't let them get away with it! Prove yourself to the nations.
See how many times I have wept as I prayed this same prayer for help.
Count them.
When you rise up against them, then I'll know you are for me!
"In God we trust"—that's our motto.
We are thankful. You have kept our feet on the right and straight path!
So we walk with you with truth and light.

Psalm 57
Great Is the Lord!

(1) Have mercy! You are safety when we are weak.
You cover us with wings as eagles. You send answers from heaven.
You hand out your love and faithfulness.
We live in a rotten culture—full of roaring lions.
Hear our praise to the skies.
Show your wonders and your power over all the earth.
(6) I felt like a trapped animal, hunted down,
but they fell into their own trap.
(7) My heart is fixed, my commitment strong.
I will sing joyfully.
Let my mind and spirit come alive.
Let all the instruments make music and wake up the world.
(9) I have a story to tell to the nations, a song to sing of your love.
How great is your love,
higher than the heavens.
Great is thy faithfulness, O God my Father.

Psalm 58

Hot Is My Anger

(1) Do you really think you're fooling us,
patronizing the courts to your own advantage?
No, we all see it plain as day.
(3) You come by it honestly—you were born with it! You brood of snakes.
Even a piping charmer cannot charm you. Go get 'em, Lord!
Tear them to shreds. Let them dry up like a creek bed.
Let their weapons be lifeless. Like slugs, like dead babies,
they will never see the light of day.
Before bramble briars catch fire and burn, they will disappear.
(10) God's people will one day be paid back in full,
splashing in the blood of cruel nations.
(11) Everyone everywhere will be saying,
"God's people have reigned again! God has judged the earth!"

Psalm 59

Deliverance

(1) This is a song of deliverance—protect us—deliver us—save us.
You see those who are set to do what is wrong.
Rise up, O God. See us as your own people. I have kept my ways pure.
The others deny and deface your goodness and grace. Show them no mercy.
(6) We hear them growling like dogs, roaming through our town.
They always stir up trouble and think nobody hears.
But I hear you laughing at them, Lord.
You are the strength of your people, my hideaway, my loving God.
(9) You will go before me and lead me to victory.
(11) I don't think your people will remember this very long
if these people are simply killed off. No, let them live with their shame
so we can see them wandering.
They have boasted so terribly about their own greatness, not yours.
Let them eat their words for all the world to see.
The world will know in every corner that you are God,
ruling your people with strength.

(16) Hear my song—each morning I will sing of your love,
for you keep me safe in the face of every trouble.
(17) O God of strength, hear my songs of praise.
You are my rock—my loving God.

Psalm 60
There Is No Winning Without the Lord

(1) We have felt your anger bursting out over us.
It tells us we have displeased you. Now we are ready to be restored.
Earthquakes have ruined the land; now we are ready to be mended.
(3) These have been tough times at your hand,
and we have learned our lessons.
But those who have been faithful now see your banner raised up for us
against those who threaten us.
Please preserve us, that your own dear ones suffer no more.
(6) Among us worshipers, God has claimed the nations:
"In victory I now own Shechem and Manasseh.
Always I proudly wear Ephraim as a helmet, hold Judah as a scepter.
Moab is my bath; Edo is my foot stool; Philistra is my pulpit."
(9) How will we take these cities for you, O God?
Isn't it you, O Lord, the same who has punished us
and shamed us in recent battles?
(11) It is you. We can only win if you are with us.
(12) So now we go forth with God to again prevail!

Psalm 61
Lead Me to the Rock

(1) Lord, listen to your children praying.
I call from every corner of the earth, even as I feel weaker than ever before.
Lead me to put my feet on the solid rock—
it's the highest that I will ever be able to reach.
(3) It has always been the Lord, the strength, the safe place.
(4) I yearn to draw close to you, Lord, and feel your loving arms.
I know you have heard my commitments

and have let me take my place with all the saints before me.
(6) I pray you let our good leaders live—and live close to you too.
(7) Show your love and faithfulness over them,
and hear my songs of joy as I keep my promises to you.

Psalm 62

In God Alone

(1) I rest when I am with God alone. My soul freedom comes from God alone. I get my strength from God alone.
God surrounds me with protection, and I cannot be shaken.
(3) How long will people tear at another person?
Will all of you turn on another because others find him struggling?
Can we kick a man when he is down?
(4) It seems people delight in tearing another down by spreading rumors.
They talk behind his back while they smile to his face.
(5) Go now; rest in God alone. Hope comes from God alone.
I get my strength from God alone.
God surrounds me with protection, and I will not be shaken.
My integrity depends on God's integrity.
(8) Make a commitment always to be honest and humble before God,
because he gives safety.
(9) We are all alike in our years allotted. We cannot add to our years.
Don't fall for easy money, though it looks so tempting.
(11) Build your life on these two truths: God is great, and God is good.
God will surely reward each of us according to what we do to live by these two truths.

Psalm 63

Streams in the Desert

(1) I am hungry for God, desperate for you, Lord.
This place is like an arid desert land without you.
(2) I have experienced you in worship places.
There, I have seen how inspiring is your power; I have heard all about how you helped people

and how your love is greater and better than life!
I'll tell my story, too, as long as I live.
I'll praise you when I gather up for worship.
I'll raise my hands in pure thankfulness.
That will feed my hungry soul. That is always a feast!
It makes me sing out loud!
(6) Lying awake at night, I will remember those good and holy moments.
You really are my strength!
I will sing while I feel your arms around me. Like a child,
I will curl up and hug you tightly.
(9) Those people who don't understand,
those who make fun of my heart for you,
they will never get past first base.
Somebody will one day shut them up and feed them to the wild animals!
(11) All the while, this person will be joyfully singing songs of praise to God.

Psalm 64

God Will Avenge

(1) Hear me; help me; hide me.
They have invaded our homeland. They conspired and struck.
(3) Their weapons were carefully honed and effective,
and their words stung just as much.
(4) It was an unexpected attack at our most vulnerable places.
How bold they were.
(5) They had been plotting together, hiding their traps,
intending death and destruction. They knew we hadn't a clue.
How clever and cruel they have been.
(7) But God will avenge. It will come just as unexpectedly.
Their lies will become their own downfall.
Everyone will know what happened, because they had it coming!
(9) Everyone will be in awe; they will acknowledge what God has done.
They will reflect on all that has happened and learn the lesson of it all.
(10) May God's people stand up and be strong in the Lord.
Let us all never give up and never stop praising the Lord.

Psalm 65

Wonderful, Wonderful God!

(1) The church will be faithful, O Lord, faithful in praise,
faithful in our commitments.
(2) Because you answer prayers, all people will one day stream to you.
(3) We were sinful, and you were forgiving.
(4) We have been chosen to serve you,
and we have never been disappointed.
You, O Lord, are great and good,
and you continually answer us with reasons to hope.
You are the hope of every corner of the world,
from sea to sea,
because of your creative power, your power over all you have created,
and your power over all history.
(8) People all over the world are hearing.
Wherever the sun rises and the evening falls,
you bring us to our feet singing with joy.
(9) You replenish the sources of land and sea.
What an abundant creation,
providing us with all we need.
You fill the creeks, soak the valleys, bless the crops.
You bless our harvest; your own provisions overflow graciously.
I can see the hillsides are smiling luxuriously.
The meadows inspire us with herds and flocks.
The valleys are draped in abundant crops.
Together, hills and valleys join in the song of joy.

Psalm 66

Wonder of Wonders

(1) Shout, sing, speak! Be joyful, everyone!
Let music tell of God's wonders. Tell the stories of God's wonders.
Let all doubters take notice and tremble!
(4) The whole earth bows before you, Lord,
singing your praises, proclaiming your wonders.
(5) So come and see! God has done it again and again,
and all of this is for us!
(6) The sea became dry, and we walked across it,
so we come forward with grateful hearts.
(7) God watches the nations, guiding and ruling.
Don't let a single doubtful soul say one word!
(8) It is time for the people to stand up and be joyful,
to really tell their stories of God.
(9) God has kept us going, kept us strong above the fray.
It was a test of what we are made of,
and we have been refined like silver in the purifying heat.
(11) God allowed it. We have been imprisoned.
We have gone through the fires and the deep waters,
but God has brought us through it all better than ever.
(13) I will keep my promise to my Lord,
all that I vowed when I was in the deepest of troubles.
I will bring my best to support the work in your name, O God.
(16) Let's get together, because I want people to hear these stories
of how God's love has made a difference in my life.
When I called upon the Lord, I praised him
with my stories of his wonders, thanking him every step of the way.
(18) If I had secrets in my heart that dishonored my God
and my commitment to live for him,
God would not have turned his hands to me. But he did.
God heard me, my prayer, and helped me.
(20) Thank you, Lord, for this wonder!
You heard my prayer; you shared your love with me.

Psalm 67
May God Bless Us

(1) May God bless us and be good to us.
May your ways be known to all the earth,
that you surround us with protective love.
(3) May God bless us and be good to us.
May the nations of the world be joyfully thankful.
You are fair, and you guide all nations.
(5) May God bless us and be good to us.
Then the land will be fruitful as God blesses us,
and all the people of every corner of this world
will join in awe and love for God.

Psalm 68
Rise Up, O Lord

(1) Let God rise up.
Let bad people run in fear, all those who deny God run in terror.
God blows them away like smoke. Like wax melting away in fire,
they die away before God.
(3) But good people are joyful when God arrives.
Sing, good people; sing, and tell God's strength.
He is Lord of all, a father to the fatherless,
a defender of widows. God is here with us.
He builds families for the lonely,
gives prisoners new hope. But God-deniers have lost their way,
finding themselves in a barren land.
(7) When you have acted for your people in need,
leading them through the wasteland,
the whole earth trembled. (9) Then you brought refreshing rains,
lifting us from our weariness.
We found our footing,
and all the poor were cared for at your hands.
(11) God spoke. God's proclaimers multiplied and passed it on.
(12) "Foreign lands and leaders run away and leave us with their bounty.

Sleep, my people. I am with you."
(14) What a blessing and what peace, knowing God is here.
(15) Rich lands watch in envy as God blesses his people by his presence.
(17) God has a well-equipped army, and it is his church.
(18) You ascended, taking prisoners,
receiving their gifts, even from the bad people.
(19) Proclaim how wonderful is God, our God,
who protects us and every day holds our troubles with us.
That's what God does!
From the God who rules the universe comes our everyday help.
(21) God is on to the bad people, the rulers who act arrogantly boastful.
"I'm coming to get you," God says,
"and I'll find you from every corner of the seven seas.
I'll wipe up the bloody mess you have made,
and even your dogs will devour the leftovers."
(24) I see God's victory lap, running right down the aisle of my church.
First are the singers and the horns and strings,
then the dance troupe of young girls.
(26) Praise is so uplifting for all God's people. Oh, praise him!
The littlest ones lead us, and the strong leaders of all,
the bright youthful faces, all are dancing down the aisles.
(28) Rise up, O God! It's a demonstration of your power and love.
You have done it so many times before.
The rulers of the nations come bearing gifts.
(30) Stop and shame the secret hiders.
Humble them till they acknowledge you.
Scatter those who rather pick fights and stir up war.
The great nations will recognize who you are and come.
(32) Sing, sing, sing! Everyone, come and sing!
This is the almighty Lord of creation—thundering in the skies.
Tell how powerful God is!
How God has helped us!
How beautifully God leads us in worship.
Say it loud! Rise up, O God!

Psalm 69

He Will Make the Weak Strong

(1) Help, Lord! I am in over my head and sinking fast!
I can't find a foothold, and the tide is rising by the minute.
I have prayed until my throat is dry, until I am going blind and crazy.
(4) People think I've really lost it, and they want to shut me up, eliminate me.
Their demands are unreasonable.
(5) You know I have made my share of mistakes—big ones!
I would be ashamed if my blunders have caused others to trip up and fall.
But I did it for your sake, Lord, though I am covered with shame.
(8) My family is embarrassed and disowns me, but I do it all
because your love is greater than all. Trusting in you is better than food!
But the news is all over town. They think I am the biggest fool around!
(13) But here I sit praying.
Because of your love and grace, you can keep me afloat,
delivering me from this shame. Don't let me sink down, please, Lord.
(16) Because of your love, because you are merciful,
come to me and do not hide.
Come quickly. I am desperate.
(19) I can't bear this scorn. I am brokenhearted and disgraced. Helpless.
Nobody has come to comfort me; instead, they ridicule me more.
(22) What they dish out must become their own miserable food.
I pray they go blind and lame, that they taste the full dose of heaven's anger.
Let them feel deserted for a change.
They have dished out plenty, blaming our loneliness on our being sinful.
They don't deserve one tiny taste of your help.
May they lose their eternal hope and be forgotten by good people.
(29) Whatever happens, my pain is very deep.
I need you more than ever, O Lord.
I am going to let my heart sing on.
I'll have a grateful heart.
I know God wants this more than a big, fat offering.
(32) Poor and needy ones will not overlook this.
They will be inspired. God will hear them loud and clear.
(34) Let heaven and earth tell of God's wonders

and every wave of the ocean be a testimony.
He never forsakes us. He will one day help us rebuild.
We will be able to bless and make the next generation secure.
Those who love God will see that God will make the weak be strong.

Psalm 70
Quickly, Lord!

(1) Quickly, Lord, to my rescue. Help me.
(2) Confuse those who try to pull me down.
Disgrace those who disgrace me.
(3) Let those who laugh at me be laughed at themselves.
(4) But let those who are genuine in their faith feel the goodness you offer
and those who love your closeness never be afraid
to speak about your goodness and love.
(5) I am worn out trying to do good, so please come quickly to me, Lord.
You alone are my strength and my hope. Quickly, Lord!

Psalm 71
I am Growing Old; Keep Me Close

(1) You are and always have been my answer to life. Keep me close to you.
Hang on to me, because you are forever good and pure.
Listen to me as I still call on you. Keep listening, hearing me still.
Just say the word, and I come to life again.
People give up on me, but you never do.
(5) I have loved you since my youth, leaned on you since my birth,
ever since my mother carried me within.
(7) I always tell others about you,
and I have encouraged many a weary soul ready to give up.
Isn't that why you made my mouth?
To keep bringing hope to people as I share your wonderful love?
(9) My days grow long and tedious, but I ask you to keep me close.
Don't think I am useless like by family now does.
The young and the restless want to move ahead and leave me out.
They say you are moving on and my old age makes me useless.

(12) That is exactly why I need you most right now.
(13) Bring down the rooftop on the people who think we are no longer useful when old.
(14) I will never quit hoping, praising, sharing,
because it never gets old, and I never run out of stories to tell.
(16) What you do gets better the more I tell it!
"The longer I serve him, the sweeter it grows!"
(17) Your voice has been a guide to me since I was young.
I can never give up on all you have taught me.
Now I am old and gray—keep me close.
Let me tell my grandchildren and the entire next generation.
(19) The purest heart, the greatest wonders, all reaching for the skies.
Who can compare with you?
(20) You have let me taste the toughest side of life,
and you always bring me back stronger.
Now that I am close to death, you still have work for me to do!
I feel honored and encouraged that you still believe I am useful.
(22) I have sung in the choir for ages now and plan to keep singing!
My mouth was made for praise because my life was made so useful to you.
My lips, my tongue, my will—
all belong to the wonderful God who made me.

Psalm 72

God's Special Leader

(1) Lord, you brought me to this position as leader over your people.
I can't do it without your blessing. I need the blessings of fair-mindedness and a pure heart.
I will discern carefully by these two standards because both are your standards and your gifts to any true leader.
(3) As grand as the mountains will be your gifts to your people.
Like the gentle and lovely hillsides will be their responsive hearts.
(4) I will defend the poor and care for their children.
I will wage a war against those who are bent on doing wrong.
(5) With your blessings, your leader can outlast them all.
Like the sun and the moon, through all the ages, he will be remembered,

Book Two: Psalms 42–72   55

fresh as rain on a new field, like showers.
(7) In his time, people will want to find goodness and wholesome living all of their days.
(8) His influence will be worldwide, strong among your people.
Primitive tribes will know him.
His enemies will come begging.
Famous leaders of other lands will honor him.
All will one day serve him.
(12) He will protect the poor who cry out to him,
the broken people of special needs.
He will genuinely care and reach out to strengthen their lives,
rescuing them from injustice and violence
because he knows their blood is precious to God.
(15) Long live God's chosen leader! Bless him!
Pray for him.
We will prosper as he leads.
We will flourish like the finest nation ever
and thrive like a well-watered field.
(17) His name will be cherished forever.
The whole world will be stronger and more peaceful because of his example.
(18) Ultimately, we will be thankful to God,
who can make such wonderful things happen for all people everywhere.
Amen!

Book Three

Psalms 73–89

Psalm 73

False Religion

(1) We all know that God is good to those who cherish goodness.
(2) But I found myself easily tempted and losing my grip.
I watched others who got rich by all their unjust schemes, and I was jealous.
(4) They were on easy street. They were physically fit,
free from the burdens of the common people, even healthier!
(6) How naturally they wore their pride.
Their lifestyles were callous and cruel to the plight of those less fortunate,
and there was no limit to it all.
(8) In their arrogance, they threaten the kindness we hold dear.
But they also are religious!
They talk about eternal life
while by their lifestyles they idolize all their possessions.
And people turn to them like they are sacred and hold all the answers.
(11) I have heard them challenge the possibility that God knows and cares.
These kinds of people act like they don't have a care in the world
as they get richer and richer.
(13) I am beginning to doubt all my efforts to stay free and pure.
I have tried to stay innocent, but I am tied up in knots of doubt and
confusion every day.
(15) Reflecting my confusion to the young people around me
would have been a travesty as befuddled as I have been.
So I went to church, and it really made sense to me.
I understood how it pans out for those smarty pants.
God spoke, telling me they were on a slippery slope,
headed for disaster. It will come quickly, and then—poof!—
they will be gone like a bad dream in God's mind.
(21) But now I am awake to this truth: I am always with you.
You never let me go.
You always speak words of wisdom. And one day you'll fulfill your promise
to bring me home eternally. Who else makes that kind of promise but you?
(26) Yes, one day I'll die; before that, I might lose confidence occasionally,
but I know where to find my confidence again.
You give me that, always and forever.

(27) Those who drift out of reach will never taste that joy
but lose it all for their unfaithfulness.
(29) But not I. Close to you is where I want to be.
You are my God and my Lord.
I'll never stop telling of your wonders.

Psalm 74

Gone Are the Sacred Retreats!

(1) What's up, Lord? We haven't heard a fresh word from you in ages.
Are you angry with your chosen flock?
(2) Remember how you chose us to be your own,
how you made us rich with your grace and mercy,
and how you made your permanent home in our midst?
(3) Turn around and look at us. We are in ruins!
Those against us have wasted your sanctuaries.
The sacred places where you have met us
have become the conference centers of wicked people.
(5) They have rearranged and overdeveloped the lovely forested hills and mountain retreats
and torn down our wonderfully meaningful places,
places to which we gave tender and sacred names.
They intentionally went after all we believe.
They would like to erase your name and memories of better days,
days when great preachers led services here and stirred our hearts.
Now we are hearing nothing at all.
(10) Lord, how long will this go on? And why do you do nothing?
You have the power to blow them away, enough even in the simple hem
of your robes.
(12) But you are my king from all generations.
You alone can liberate us.
We remember the Red Sea. You split it wide open.
You eliminated monsters in the deep and fed them to animals of the desert.
(15) The whole creation is yours.
You started the flowing creeks and rivers and dried them up at your disposal.
Days and nights all belong to you, just like the sun and the moon.

(17) You set the boundaries of the earth.
You made the seasons—summer, fall, winter, and spring.
Yet the doubters, proud of themselves,
tease those of us who would credit you with all of this.
(19) I beg of you: do not give up on us and hand us over to them,
like a dove to an animal. We are broken, but we are yours still.
(20) It is the covenant we made that holds us together,
don't forget, because the darkness of violent people seems so near.
We are a fearful people, but don't let us run away.
May we always honor your goodness and grace.
(22) But we depend on you, Lord, for the protection of honorable things,
your things. Rise up, Lord!

Psalm 75

God Always Has the Final Word

(1) We are full of thankfulness because we feel your presence with us.
All around us are people who can testify to your loving kindness.
(1) You said, "It is I who sets the times and the seasons
when people's lives face judgment, and I alone will judge fairly.
(3) When terror strikes at the heart of good people,
they remain because I will it to be. I begat you!"
(4) So to the self-sufficient who think they are gods, I say, "Stop your bragging."
To people who live to make up their own rules as they go along, I say, "Not so fast, you fools!
Beware of tooting your own horns and yelling out your almighty opinions!"
(6) Not one of us dares to put another person on a pedestal.
God alone will choose who succeeds or who flounders.
It just seems God holds a cup of intoxicating drink, and every fool in town
gobbles it up. What fools!
(9) Not so for me. Whatever it costs, I will keep trusting and worshiping
the one who has the final word.
God says, "Fools will choke on their silly self-pride.
Songs of joy sung by good people will never be silenced."

Psalm 76
God Rules the Nations

(1) God's people know God well. No guesswork for them!
And we know the majesty and greatness of our God.
(2) He is here with us in his church,
right here among the people who love him.
He has overcome those who have threatened us with war.
(4) Lord, you shine brightly, more wonderfully than anything in all creation.
(5) Brave men and women have given their lives in war,
but when it's over, it's over.
When God calls it off, everybody is silent.
(7) We should always remember that you rule the nations.
Who can face you when you have had enough?
(8) You boomed forth about winners and losers,
and the nations finally quieted down.
When you made the call on the side of the downtrodden, that was it.
(10) Truly, your absolute fairness makes us all stand to our feet and cheer.
All who can live through that finally get quiet!
(11) People, listen! Make commitments to the Lord your God,
and keep them right down to the last period.
Let all the nations do the same.
Give them room to honor God in their own way too.
(12) God has provided! True kings and leaders recognize
that God alone is Lord!

Psalm 77
God Is Great, and God Is Always Good

(1) Maybe I cry out to God too much.
Maybe I am always whining, complaining day and night.
(3) It is simply because I know how you work, Lord,
what power you have, how you have helped me,
how you have guided me in the past. That makes me cry all the more.
(6) With songs in the night, days gone by,
you kept me awake and heard my lonely prayers.

(7) Today I sound just like I did back then:
"Will the Lord ignore me?
Will he never come to my aid with his love?
Can't I take a turn at winning and being on top once in a while?
What happened to the promise?
What happened to mercy?
What happened to compassion?
Is God angry with me?"
(10) But I changed my tune:
"I will remember the good days,
the days when God remembered me. There have been miracles.
There have been great moments when I was sure you heard me,
all of us, and all of your beloved people. (13) All God's ways are perfect,
and there is none like you—not one!
Miracles! Power! Forgiveness! Grace!
You have always remembered us, even when we forget you!
(16) At your display of power,
the seas became stormy;
the heavens rained; we heard thunder and saw lightning!
Everybody heard it everywhere and ran for cover!

Psalm 78

A List of God's Works

(1) This is the teaching about God's good works so no one will forget.
Listen up, everybody.
(2) I will speak in story form, in moralizing tales.
You will recognize that this is ancient wisdom,
things you have heard from your grandparents.
(4) The next generation deserves to hear the great works of God.
(5) God laid down life principles for our forefathers,
and these became laws for the land,
which God required us to pass along, generation to generation.
(6) All generations will know, including those not yet born.
(7) It is all about trusting in God,
never forgetting God's great works,

keeping all God's teachings.
(8) This is to avoid the mistakes of the past,
when people were stubborn as mules,
ornery, and disobeyed God, even unfaithful to their promises.
(9) Remember how the warriors of Ephraim were armed to the teeth,
yet ran away like cowards. They had not kept God's covenant
and had refused all these life principles.
(11) They had forgotten that God was trustworthy,
that God had done great things to provide for them.
(12) God had performed miracles—rescuing them from Egypt.
(13) God had split the Red Sea and led them through it.
(14) God had created a cloud to guide them in daylight
and a firelight during the nighttime.
(15) God had split rocks in the desert,
and water so abundant had rushed forth for their needs.
Everywhere they went, God made more water available.
(17) None of that mattered to them.
They still chose to do as they pleased.
They whined for more and challenged God.
(19) When they did not get their way, they complained that God
did not care.
Water wasn't enough. Now they wanted T-bone steaks.
"We deserve it! Won't God deliver?!"
(21) Finally, when God had had enough, he broke out in angry and fiery ways.
(23) Yet God continued his marvelous provisions.
When God spoke, heaven opened up and dropped holy manna
to keep people well fed.
(26) God controlled the far winds from every corner,
all for their benefit. In fact, the T-bone steak did come, so to speak.
There were game birds aplenty, inside the camp and out,
raining down like a dust storm or sands on the seashore.
(27) "Good food, good meat! Good God, let's eat!"
This was their motto, but before they had swallowed what they had,
God struck back.
Many leaders and strong young people were struck down.
(32) So you think they got the message? No way.

They kept doing it their way, so God cut off the blessings;
the gravy train came to a screeching halt.
They suddenly felt the futility of their ways, and they were finally terrified.
(34) Isn't it sad? Whenever God struck them, they would listen, eagerly
turning toward him.
They clung to the rock of God;
they remembered how merciful God had been.
But it was all talk. That beauty was only skin deep.
Their hearts had not changed.
(38) Again, with mercy, God was forgiving. God spared them.
Time and time again, God spared them.
(39) God was gentle with them; weak and breezy were they.
(40) The story goes on and on.
They snubbed God in the desert and broke God's heart while they wandered.
They challenged God, antagonized God, forgot God,
and they forgot how God had performed miracles for them.
(44) How God turned their rivers to blood, undrinkable!
How God sent swarms of flies that ate them up
and frogs that overwhelmed them.
(46) How God gave their crops over to grasshoppers
and their vegetables to the locusts.
(47) God sent the freezes and hailstorms to destroy vineyards,
fig trees, cattle herds, and all their livestock.
It seemed unbelievably merciless, but anyone who knows God
would have recognized that God's patience has its limits
and his anger is justified.
God even sent plagues, and the high price was death.
(51) Egypt lost their first born to these plagues.
Ham saw theirs dying off as well.
Still, the faithful got a pass.
They had God's shepherding love guiding into those
"green pastures and still waters," like God had promised.
(54) They were led right up to the rim of that "holy land,"
the place God had prepared by clearing off pagan nations.
It was the inheritance of the faithful!
(56) But as if none of this had happened,

Book Three: Psalms 73–89

the people soon backslid into their old ways,
ignoring those protective "guides of God."
No different from their ancestors, they acted "privileged"
rather than "responsible"!
God was furious. He had had it with these faithless scoundrels, because they tested him!
(60) God left the church—empty—
the very place he had promised to meet them as they prayed.
(61) God let the enemy raid their safe spots and steal their sacred relics.
Imagine the enemy wearing our crosses.
(62) Then God let the enemy raid the people,
because he was just that angry.
Very few weddings—honorable ones—were held.
There was nothing about love to celebrate.
Preachers were dragged out and killed.
Women became numb to the terrors, and no one even cried anymore.
(65) But again, there was a limit even to that anger of God.
And God woke up, like a drowsy, drunken warrior.
He rose up and took back the land, threshing those shameful enemies.
Even the families of Joseph's lineage were put to shame.
Yet God chose the families of Judah whom he loved.
(69) Again, God raised up a beautiful sanctuary high on a hill for all to see,
strong as the earth itself.
(70) And God selected a faithful shepherd boy, right from the hills,
and made him to shepherd God's chosen people of love,
like his own family.
(72) Now we can see all the great ways and works of God.
David became "a man after God's own heart."
He ruled by shepherding God's people—
pure of heart, unselfish, skillful.
What a leader!
And God did it all! Amen!

Psalm 79

When God Is Angry, Nobody Wins

(1) O God, it's the pagan nations again!
They have invaded our sacred inheritance, your land.
They captured the temple, made it theirs,
and blew up all the sacred historical sites in the city.
(2) It gets worse. Like animals, they hunt and shoot down your people
and leave them in the streets to be eaten by the wild animals.
Blood flows in the streets.
There aren't enough healthy people left to bury all the dead.
(4) Neighboring lands say we deserved it, and they laugh.
(5) It's your disgust with us and our ways.
But how long can you let it go on? Until we are wiped out?
(6) Turn it on the enemy for a change, the unbelievers,
the pagan, corrupt lands,
because they have all but wiped us off the face of the earth.
(8) Think how these other nations will stop and see our power and glory
if you forgive us.
(10) How can we let them keep saying,
"Now where is their self-designed, pretend God?"
You must do it, God; you must avenge all your chosen people.
Can you hear the groans of your people in prison?
You can release them if you will, especially those on death row.
(12) Come get these nasty nations of sin.
Give them seven times their due,
seven times what they have dished out against your wonderful record.
(13) Lord, your people want to praise you again in inspiring worship,
like we always have done.
First, it will take your strong arm to silence their arrogance
and to smash their pride so we can be confident and joyful to worship you.

Psalm 80

We Call Upon the Lord, Our God

(1) We call upon you who have shepherded this people like a prize herd,
like the king of Heaven, who sits enthroned between the angels,
before all nations.
(3) **Restore our lost prominence with your shining glory.**
We feel your displeasure.
Our only identity is to be a weeping people, so forlorn and forgotten
that all nations consider us as most pitiful of them all.
(7) **Restore our lost prominence with your shining glory.**
(8) We are your vineyard, set free from slavery,
a new field cleared, then planted.
You rooted us, and we have grown.
The entire mountains have rested in the shade you created with us.
We are like the mighty cedar trees of the land, stretching out to the sea,
planting our own seeds all the way to the river banks.
(12) But you have given up on us and let us grow weak
and picked at by every Tom, Dick, and Harry.
Now we are exposed to every crazy idea that comes along.
(14) Come back to the heart of your people, Lord.
We are your vine; come back from heaven and tend to us.
(16) The vine now is down, laid low at your hand.
Give power to your chosen leader for us; then we will not resist.
Renew our hearts, and we will learn to pray and depend on you again.
(19) **Restore our lost prominence with your glorious, shining strength.**
All we need is your glory shining on us again.

Psalm 81

Because God Can Make a Way

(1) Let the music play! Sing about the strength of our God.
Shout, shake, strum whatever you have,
because God calls on us to face the future with fresh courage.
(6) Listen to his promise: "I pulled you out of slavery.
I heard you when you called.

I answered you with storms, and you were tested by the seaside.
(8) Listen, and I will show you how to grow strong.
The way is through the purity of your heart. Will this one thing, that I alone can be your God.
You saw how I set you free once before. Open your hearts,
and I will do it again.
(11) But all this fell on deaf ears. My people were too busy.
Suddenly I was a stranger to them! So I let them go their own way.
(13) If my people would heed what I have been teaching through the years,
how quickly my strength would make a way for them.
The haughty and mouthy ones would shrink away,
and they would get what they have had coming to them.
(16) "Not you," God says.
"You would have a feast waiting, 'honey from the rock'!"

Psalm 82

Hear Ye! Hear Ye! Court Is Now in Session!

(1) Imagine God holding court among all the little gods
we have set up to worship.
I can see it now. He lights into them: "How's this being 'rich and famous' working for you?
Rubbing elbows with the elite?
(3) I'll say again what I have said many times before: (4) 'Rescue the perishing, care for the dying, snatch them in pity from sin and the grave!'
See the ones that I see: weak, fatherless, sore, and
(5) oppressed. I see them as so needy, ready for you to deliver them.
But they act like they have never heard a word I said, and they enjoy it!
Ignorance is blind. All the while, the very pillars of the earth are crumbling.
I've implored them: 'You are made in my very image!'
But you have a limited time, like every other human,
and so will every proud ruler."
(8) Rise up, O God! Hold court. Every nation belongs to you.
We wait for your excellent judgments!

Psalm 83

Holy Silence Doesn't Cut It

(1) Lord, your silence is driving us nuts!
No, silence is *not* golden in our context!
Ramp it up! Stir it up!
(2) Your enemies can do that, and they're getting away with it!
How slick are their subtle plans behind closed doors.
They're planning to erase all the good that was done
before they came to power.
(4) "Let's wipe out their memory," they are saying.
"God's era of God's people will be faint and forgotten."
(5) They are powerfully single-minded,
making alliances with all kinds of disgruntled groups
whose selfish anger has been simmering for generations.
(8) Even the wealthy barons of industry have thrown in millions
to sway the votes their way.
(9) Lord, you have cleansed this land before. Do it again.
(10) In days gone by, your enemies never got away with this treachery.
They ran out of resources; their leaders all became intolerably corrupt.
They bragged of developing your lands put aside for your people.
But no, they and their plans fizzled out like dry brush.
(13) Do it again, Lord. Like a forest fire or a dust bowl,
unleash your grapes of wrath.
Put them to shame. Let your people be encouraged to seek you
and honor you again.
(18) Let them know who is in charge.
Your name is above every name.
Let them hear that loud and clear.

Psalm 84

There's No Better Place Than the Church

(1) I look at the sanctuary and am overcome! You made this God's house,
and it is lovely to me.
(2) Deep inside I crave to gather there quietly,

because my whole body yearns to be close to you, Lord.
(3) I watch even the tiny sparrow finding peace and building a nest right here.
She can have her little ones safely, right near your altar.
O Lord! You are the prince of peace. You are God!
(4) Blessed are all of us who find our strength here.
Everyone can feel the joy rising within as they make their way to your church.
(6) When troubles come on the road to church, it actually feels like a blessing.
A rainy day even brings sunlight!
(7) One by one, people gain strength at every turn on the way to church
until that front door opens and someone greets them
with a "Welcome!" and a hug!
(8) We come to pray, Lord. Hear us.
We come to unburden our souls, Lord. Please welcome us.
(9) Remember that we are your own family as we come in,
and give us that warm and badly needed embrace.
(10) It is poetry, and it's true:
"Better is one day in your courts than a thousand elsewhere!
I would rather be a doorkeeper in the house of my God"
than stay as a guest in the lavish home of someone
who thinks they are a self-made person!
(11) Because our God is light and strength,
our Lord loves and blesses his people with grace undeserved.
He holds nothing back from us when we love to walk close to him.
(12) I just cannot say enough! "My Lord and my God!"
Blessed are all of us who really trust in you.

Psalm 85

Welcome Back, Sons and Daughters

(1) How sweet is your forgiveness, Lord.
The whole body of your people is redeemed,
renewed when you wash us clean and give us a fresh start.
Your anger is deserved, but you have ceased now.
(4) Do it again, Lord! We can't bear knowing we have brought shame to
your family name.
Revive our wilted spirits. Let us sing joyfully again.

(7) It is your love that we long to experience.
It makes us whole again just to touch the hem of your garment.
(8) We hear your promises, and we long for that peace.
(9) We know you can never be far from us, or far from blessing us,
because your mighty power will be seen over us.
(10) It is a homecoming dream
that your love and the faithfulness of your people share a joyful gathering.
I can see it now.
In your patient and passionate fatherhood, you see us coming a long way off.
You run to meet us and welcome us back from the far country.
You embrace us. You kiss us. We're home again.
(12) You kill the fatted calf. You call for a celebration:
"My sons and daughters have been lost, but now they are found."
(13) Your good name precedes you, Lord. We are prepared for you!

Psalm 86

What Becomes of the Broken-Hearted?

(1) It's another blue Monday, Lord, and here I am praying.
I am a broken person again, poor and needy.
(2) You are my hope and my help. You are all I have and all I want.
It is mercy that I need, and with this gift will come my joy.
When it comes down to mercy, you never fail.
You hear even "the least of these" and answer with love.
(7) I call in trouble, and you hear me.
(8) Among all the things we mortals worship, there is none like you, Lord.
Nothing compares with your work of love.
(9) One day all nations will bow down and bend their knees
to God our Father.
(10) It is you, Lord, all the way.
(11) I am a sponge; teach me. I am a child; hold me tight.
I am a follower. I am a servant.
(13) I have come to worship. You are my Savior.
(14) The proud ridicule my honesty and my humility.
(15) Yet your compassion and your grace call me home again.
You are patient, loving, and faithful.

(16) Come, O Lord, with fresh mercy. My weak and broken heart
needs your strong power of healing, just as I learned at my mother's knee.
(17) Raise your banner of love over me again,
that those who do not understand
might see and be drawn to you also.
My help and my hope are in you, Lord.

Psalm 87

God Chose the Church

(1) God set out to establish one place where everyone could come into his holy presence.
He found it in the church.
God loves it more than all the traditions of the past,
(3) and people everywhere are abuzz about its great days.
(4) "The nations are mine, but when I choose a leader,
it will be one whom I have known from a child.
People everywhere will tell the difference, and say,
'Look what a difference a church can make in someone's life.'
(6) The Lord never forgets those he has known from childhood.
The glorious music that pours forth from the church will be singing,
'All the gifts of God are in his church!'"

Psalm 88

Depression

(1) O God, who shepherds me 24/7, I now cry out to you.
I know you hear my prayers. Now hear my darkest crying as well.
(3) Deep down, I am depressed! I would rather be dead.
(4) I am as good as dead since I have not the strength to get going.
I might as well be dead among the mortally wounded
who are left behind, because there is no hope for me.
I am like those dead who no longer can feel your presence.
I believe you have brought me to this point.
I believe I have lived so desperately wrong
that you have just left me for dead in your anger.
(8) It is you who have separated me from close friends
and made me impossible to them.
I am backed into a corner with my impossible sense of doom.
Who would want to be around me? I don't blame them!
This is why I cry out to you, Lord, the healer of all.
When we die, we can't rejoice in you. All is over.
Has anyone ever come back from the dead to be a witness to your love?
Anybody ever laid cold in the grave and declared your compassion to the others who are dead?
Once we are dead, does it matter? Would we care?
(13) This is why I cry out to you, Lord, 24/7.
Why can I not hear or see you?
I have been struggling with this darkness since I was young.
It has been a dark, dark struggle.
I feel your angry look. I feel it is your anger that darkens my mind.
(17) I feel like I am drowning in despair, going down, down, down.
(18) When my family is all gone and my friends desert me,
my only companion is my depression.

Psalm 89

O God, Remember the Covenant

(1) "I have no greater song to sing than of God my king.
To him my praise I bring. Forevermore."
(2) God's love never changes.
God's faithful character is evidenced in the heavens.
How could I sing of lesser things?
God made a pledge with a man of his heart—David.
David was God's chosen line; his rule will last for all the generations.
(5) Heaven declares your artistry and reminds us as we worship
that you are faithful, and you call us to be holy, as you are.
(6) No one in the heavens can compare with the Lord.
(7) Respect can be felt among the leaders of God.
All know then that nobody can touch that.
(8) Strength, power, and amazing faithfulness are your mantle.
(9) You rule the seas. You calm the storms at sea.
You always prevail over pretended rulers and arrogant nations,
because you created it all and all that is within it.
(12) You created North and South, and both sing your glories.
(13) Your people are strong. Your name is strong. Your worship is uplifting.
(14) You rule by goodness, purity, and fairness,
and you back it up with the greatest love. You are unchanging.
(15) We are so happy to belong to you.
You make us joyfully confident as we fall with your truths,
and your very companionship is a constant parade of joy.
(17) Because you are generous, you have entrusted all creation,
plus the quality of your character, to us.
We are yours. You are the king of creation and of this created caregiver body.
(19) You gave this vision, entrusted it to your people:
"I gave my strength to one warrior, one young man.
It is David my servant, anointed with oil, sustained by my own hand,
strengthened by my people—his people.
(22) No fools can mock him; no enemy can take him out.
I will handle the opposition and remove his antagonists.
(24) The banner he flies will be my love,

and unlimited resources will come due by my own reputation.
(25) He will rule the seas. He will command the rivers.
He will pray, 'My Father, my rock, my savior.'
He will be my only begotten son, highest above all kings and rulers.
My love will never be withheld from him or from his own kind.
(29) And I will ensure this promise as long as the heavens endure.
(30) If his people fail me, they will bear the consequences,
but I will never withhold my love. I will never be unfaithful.
I will neither break my promises nor change my mind.
(35) This is my pledge to my chosen one—David.
His line will stand forever over my people.
Like sun and moon, their reign will never fail."
(38) But something has changed;
something of your covenant love has been turned off.
The rulership you promised is now tarnished, defiled, broken.
(40) Our walls are broken down, our strength diminished,
our resources plundered, our reputation squandered.
(42) Suddenly our enemies are proudly waving their flags over us
because we have floundered and failed in important battles.
You have not come through for us
and instead have chosen our tormentors.
We have become ashamed.
(46) Is this to continue forever?
Is this the way it is to be?
(47) We are truly fragile, and life itself is fleeting for all persons everywhere.
None of us escapes death, the final enemy.
Where is the promise of love you gave to David?
(50) Look at our shame. Look how it breaks our hearts in two.
Listen to what they say. They shame us, and they shame you.
(52) "Though he slay me, yet will I praise him!"
Amen and amen.

Book Four

Psalms 90–106

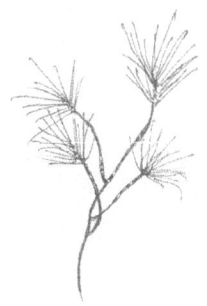

Psalm 90

An Ancient Reflection and Prayer

(1) Lord, you have been home to us, a place of refuge and safety,
for lo these many years.
You are God; never should we doubt! (2) You existed before mountains
or the whole earth and this world. For all eternity you are God!
(3) After all we attempt, you bring us back to the dust of the earth simply
by calling to us, "Come home, my people."
(4) A thousand years in your time is just like another passing day
or one incredible evening.
(5) You erase the slate of our lives. We spring up like daily grasses
and wilt by evening.
(7) We are terrified by your holy perfection,
and we vanish when you call in the cards.
(8) Our prideful wrongs flash before your eyes,
and nothing is kept secret from your shining presence.
(9) Our days answer to your laws,
and we groan on the way to the grave, each one of us.
(10) Though we know we have no more than seventy years, possibly eighty if we stay healthy,
yet we make trouble and heartache. Then, suddenly, our time is up, and our lives are over.
(11) Could it be your holiness becomes so offended by our ways
that it consumes even our feeble attempts to respect you?
(12) Show us how to make every day count
that we might gain the wisdom necessary to live lives of significance.
(13) Lord, please stop this meaningless merry-go-round.
Show compassion here.
Bless us each morning with your sweet love
that we might sing with joy each and every day.
(15) Help us understand our troubles—the little ones and the big ones—
in light of your bigger picture.
(16) Help us to be authentic in our witness of all you have done
so we may pass on your magnificent power to the next generation.
(17) We pray for your blessings, O Lord our God.

Make good of all we try to do.
Yes, turn our poor human attempts into something that makes a difference.

Psalm 91
Close to Thee, Close to Thee

(1) If you stay close to God, you will find the peace that passes all understanding.
(2) I can attest to the power of the Lord.
He protects me, and I will always trust him.
(3) I know he will save you from the traps of our culture,
from the temptations that can ruin you.
(4) God covers his own people like a dove protects her young with her wings.
It is because he never changes. That is your security.
(5) The darkness holds nothing to fear for you
nor the open threats of the daily grind.
(6) Even disease and calamity cannot threaten you.
(7) Watch the multitudes stumble, the throngs fail utterly,
but none of this can threaten your life.
(8) You may see it all around
and witness the consequences that fall on the guilty.
(9) But if you stay close to the Lord,
nothing can harm you.
(11) The angels will be called up to be your guard.
(12) They will lift you in their hands and hold you securely.
The stones, the snakes, the wild animals—
all will fall to your strength.
(14) "Because he or she loves me," says the Lord, "I will keep them safe.
I will hold them close because they have stayed close to me.
He or she will pray, and I will answer.
I will stay close in good and bad times and honor them through it all.
(16) I will bestow long life upon them and, in the end,
give them eternal life."

Psalm 92

How Great Is Our God

(1) Every opportunity to praise our God is so rewarding,
and every song lifts our souls.
(2) We can proclaim your great love in the morning as we awaken
and your amazing faithfulness in the evening.
We can use every stringed instrument available, every person,
and still barely begin to express all the joy in our hearts, O Lord.
(4) Oh, how happy you have made me! Oh, how happy you have made me!
Your working in my life is the greatest gift, so undeserved,
and I sing deep down in my soul.
(5) Words can hardly express the greatness of your thoughts;
how foolish are those who deny it.
When they assail the great works of proud and arrogant people,
they show their ignorance about how small
and soon forgotten are such people.
(8) Not you, Lord.
Your praises will never cease to be heard throughout the land,
while fools pass off unnoticed.
(10) While I sing, you give me strength like a wild buffalo.
Lavish gifts are given. Wonders are observed. Enemies are defeated.
The sounds of battle are over.
(12) How lovely are your people, Lord.
They flourish like well-cared-for palms and cedars that adorn your chosen
houses of worship.
They stand tall in your sanctuaries.
(14) As they age, they grow richer, staying fresh, bringing forth good fruits.
We keep singing that our God is holy and pure
and perfect in all his ways.
He is a rock and anchor in life to us all.

Psalm 93
Endless Praise

(1) The Lord is sovereign, ruling all history,
robed in the majesty of his creation,
expressed in the power of all creation.
The world without end is God's creation.
(2) It is all your throne from which you reign.
It began before we ever imagined or shared this life. You are eternal.
(3) Every ocean is a joyful chorus,
every pounding wave a storage of grace.
Yet you are mightier than the waters or any part of creation can express!
(5) Your principles for loving cannot be matched.
Your beauty and perfection are the theme of our church.
We will sing your endless praise for endless days, O Lord!

Psalm 94
We Shall Overcome Some Day

(1) O Lord, O God, to whom vengeance belongs, shine forth.
(2) Rise up, O judge of all the earth. Pay back, avenge
all who think they own this world.
We cannot bear to hear their loud self-aggrandizement much longer.
How repulsive is their boasting,
and they never miss an opportunity to claim credit for anything
and everything good.
(5) They belittle and humiliate those of us who love and trust you, Lord.
They have no mercy for widows, for immigrants, for orphaned children.
They say, "People deserve what they have gotten in life.
If there was a God, this God would have helped."
(8) I am warning all you who brag of power and wealth.
Your ignorance is showing.
"The emperor has no clothes."[1]
How can you say God doesn't hear when it is God
who makes ears and forms eyes?

Do you imagine that the God who made the nations will not allow consequences of punishment?
Can you conceive of a God who teaches understanding not having knowledge himself?
Oh yes, God knows all our thoughts,
and he knows how small and futile they are.
(12) How happy is the person you discipline like your own child, Lord.
These persons now may learn your life principles and
learn to avoid the stupidity of poor life choices.
One day the fools of this world will fall in the grave they have been digging.[1]
(14) You never neglect your people, Lord.
We belong to you by your own choice.
We can see what is right in life by the wonder of your own judgments.
We can see and follow these ourselves.
(16) Where are the statesmen of our generation? Who will stand with us?
Unless God had raised up new leaders, I would have died a lonely death.
(18) As sure as I cried that my footing in truth was giving way,
right then I felt your love surround me!
When I panicked, your promises brought joy within my heart.
(20) Can a corrupt ruler be at home with you, Lord? One who ignores basic human rights and dignity?
There are so many who lay claim to be in absolute power while they crush the common people,
ignore the right to health care for all.
(22) Our God will not ignore this. God will repay these sinful rulers,
and they shall be wiped away.
We shall overcome some day.
Oh, deep in my heart, I do believe, we shall overcome some day.[2]

[1] Line from fable by Hans Christian Andersen.

[2] Pete Seeger, "We Shall Overcome."

Psalm 95

With the Voice of Singing

(1) Come with a voice of singing;
let's proclaim God's love and mighty power.
Our music and our songs will tell of God's mighty work in our lives
and our thankfulness to God.
(3) The Lord whom we love is the almighty God, the king above all that
thrills us in our life.
(4) Our God has the whole world in his hands.
He has the wide-flowing waters in his hands.
He has the whole world in his hands.
(6) Come, let us bow down in worship;
let us kneel before the Lord our maker,
for he alone is God, and we are the people of his pasture,
the flock he tenderly cares for.
Today, if you hear his voice, do not withdraw in selfish pride,
as you have done when feeling threatened before
or when you faced some formidable obstacle
and thought you could test God like so many have done before.
Though some have tried, it has never worked for them.
(10) You know the history;
my anger was kindled against foolish generations of the past,
forty years for some.
My word to them and now to you is that they made a path
apart from my ways,
thinking they knew better.
It only led them down a path of destruction.
(11) I had to let them go because I am a God of freedom.
My anger had hardly been as hot as in those days.
My word to them loudly proclaimed,
"You will never find the peace I have created for you and promised to you
when you go that way apart from me."

Psalm 96

God Is the Mighty King of Love

(1) Sing with all your might about God's love.
Make it a new song, fresh from your heart.
Sing about God's mercy, God's grace,
God's goodness and loving kindness.
Tell the whole world it is free grace—grace to all in need.
(4) It is the greatness of God of which we sing.
Respect him above everything else that you cherish.
All pales in comparison.
Everything else is passing, but God is the creator of all things.
(6) It is marvelous, all that God has done. It is magnificent,
all that God provides within his church and among his people.
(7) Give God the respect due his name.
Cherish the wonder of his strength available to us.
Bring your offerings and come singing, praising, rejoicing in the wonder of his perfect love.
Let all this surrounding creation tremble as God rises up over all.
(10) Tell all nations; don't keep it from them.
God's ways in the world will never change.
He watches and knows us, and he judges all people with equal fairness.
(11) Let all heaven sing. Let all the earth smile and be glad.
Join in, oceans and all you fish and water beasts.
Join in, farm lands and all growing crops from within.
Join in, forest, and hear the trees singing.
(13) When God walks on the earth, all creation will sing,
for he will bring peace and fairness finally one day.
God will judge us everyone by his mercy and truth.

Psalm 97

Lord of All the Earth

(1) The Lord is in control of creation, rest assured,
so let's be confident and joyful.
Even the faraway places know his truth and share our confident hope.

(2) When God moves among us, it seems stormy because we cannot know him or know his ways,
but we can trust that goodness and mercy are behind all that he does.
(3) When God moves among us, it seems the world is aflame
as he blazes through all the evils of this world.
(4) I have seen him in the lightning, heard him in the thunder, and felt him in the rain.
My God is near me all the time.
(7) Those who make idols of their possessions are ultimately disappointed,
so worship God with those things you call God!
(8) Your people will stay vigilant and joyful, O Lord,
because you always deal with us fairly. Every day you prove to us why you are God of all the earth.
(10) We have our orders:
If you love the Lord of all the earth, you must be clearly against what is wrong, what is evil.
God will protect you as you stand up.
(11) God will share his truth within your heart.
God will bring you joy when you stand tall for what is right.
(12) So rejoice, ye pure in heart! Lift up your voice to praise the Lord of all the earth!

Psalm 98

The Sweet Song of Salvation

(1) It is time to sing, time to make melody in our hearts,
because God has done wonders of his grace.
(2) God has let us see a larger picture of his holy plan.
God has let the nations see his power.
God has activated his covenant of love and unchanging grace to his own chosen people.
And everyone has seen it, knows it, trusts it, fears it!
(4) It is time to shout, time to be joyful with our music,
to use every instrument available: guitars, organs, flutes, violins,
horns of every shape and size, even the ram's horn!
All of it is due God's glorious love.

(7) Let the oceans join in, and all that swim.
Let the world join in, and all who live upon it.
Let the rivers rush with happy sounds.
(9) Let them all sing about God's wonders,
for he is coming in pure power and love.
God comes to claim his own
while everything will experience God's majestic power and perfect purity.
God is fair to all!

Psalm 99

That's Why We Sing

God is surrounded by angels. Let the earth be amazed and respectful.
God is great; God is good. Let us thank him as we should.
(3) Everybody sing out—God is good!
(4) God's power is in his hand with sure fairness
and equal consideration of all.
Through your church you have shown that your kingdom is based on just treatment of all.
(5) That's why we sing and shout the victory.
(6) Our spiritual forefathers prayed and called upon you, Lord.
Since you faithfully answered them, they taught us how to trust and obey,
for there is no other way.
You led and thrilled Moses and Aaron;
you taught Samuel by signs and wonders.
In obedience to your word, the happiness, the answers that fixed their faith.
You have always graciously forgiven your people,
and you have let us off the hook; the consequences of their wrongs still had to be borne!
Because you are the Lord, good and true,
we gather in your sacred places to fellowship with you and one another.

Psalm 100
Doxology—Thanksgiving

(1) Gather up joyfully, tell out wonderfully, the Lord is Lord of all.
Let your gathering be sheer gladness—come with songs and awe and wonder.
(3) Experience God. God made us.
We belong to him, his people, the sheep of his own pasture.
(4) Step into his presence with a heart full of thankfulness,
and that will give you an endless song to sing.
Thanksgiving is good. God is good.
God's love is forever good.
God will always be good to every generation.

Psalm 101
Purity—To Will One Thing[1]

(1) He keeps me singing; my songs are about the wonderful love of God.
The justice of our God keeps me singing songs of praise.
(2) But I, too, will lead a blameless life, that God will come to me in my need.
Nothing beats the good feeling from doing what is right!
Accordingly, I will not entertain the trash in our society.
It is only a trap, easy to fall into, and the downward slide is fast.
And I hate to see when someone gets trapped!
(4) I will be careful about the friends I choose.
I will steer clear of those who tempt me.
(5) Neither will I listen to the gossipers. I will shut them up quickly.
And the smug ones who act like they don't need anybody—I'm staying away!
(6) I'm joining up with the good people who try to do right.
They are as good for me as I can be for them.
(7) Not so for the dishonest and deceitful.
If they're playing loose with the truth, I'm calling them out.
(15) This is my daily creed, my promise to myself and to my God.
I want to be pure and good,
and I want to keep this land of ours pure for the Lord!
Amen.

[1] Title of devotional classic by Søren Kierkegaard.

Psalm 102

A Word for the Destitute

(1) I am praying from seeing and feeling the darkness of despair.
I know you hear me. Let this prayer be a plea for all who are destitute.
Our pain and misery are unbearable.
(3) The days pass so quickly, like smoke from my campfire,
and my bones are like the glowing embers, furious but soon to grow cold.
I have no desire to live, no motivation to even eat my food.
Nobody wants to hear my agony. It drives them away,
and none stays close enough to encourage me.
(6) I feel like that lonely one who sits alone
overlooking the parched desert land.
I remember the stark image of a lonely bird on the wires overhead.
(8) I have always spoken up with such faith that the scoffers now have the upper hand.
The critics, the cynics, the doubters say, "Who's sorry now? Who wants to be like him?"
(9) My food is tasteless; nothing I drink can satisfy this great,
dark loneliness I feel.
It is you, Lord, who has ignored me.
(11) Look at the evening shadows,
and see how similar are my last fading hopes.
I bend low like the grasses in the evening.
(12) Yet this is our hope taught through the ages:
that you never change, sitting on your throne, a reputation for grace throughout every generation.
(13) I know you will soon rise up with compassion for your own people,
for it is high time to raise us up along with you: "Now is the day of salvation!"
(14) Every church house we have built is a precious remembrance of our sustaining grace.
Even when reduced to rubble, our church buildings inspire us.
All nations have heard of your grace
and truth, and their rulers envy your passion and power.
(16) You will build us, and you will shine for all the world again.

Book Four: Psalms 90–106

You answer the prayers of the weakest among us.
You have never ignored the destitute.
(18) Let these be our sacred writings that new generations yet unborn
may be among the gloriously joyful people of praise: "God will see us!
From his throne in the high heavens, he sees the earth, hears the prisoners,
and sets free those condemned to die."
(21) Let God's goodness and grace be our theme
and his praises fill our sanctuaries.
(23) I once was destitute myself. My time was limited, and my health and
strength were ebbing away.
(24) So I prayed to live: "Please, Lord, let me finish my life's work,
my vision, my dreams.
You are God for all eternity. You began the life with the laying of the
foundations of the earth.
Then you flung the stars in space. The creation will pass away,
but you will live on.
The creation is like a garment to clothe your amazing grace.
When you no longer need them, like old clothes, you will toss them all away.
But not you, Lord. You are for all eternity, and forever the same.
(28) We pledge our families to you, to live in praise and adoration,
forever close to you.
And every generation to follow will be taught the old, old story.

Psalm 103

My Highest Praise

(1) How glorious is my God.
Let every fiber of my being sing out the wonder of his grace.
(2) Say it and sing it again, and don't forget all the ways God has touched
this life of mine.
(3) God has forgiven my sins; God has healed all my diseases;
God has taken the sting out of death,
and God has us as subjects of his amazing love and constant compassion.
(5) As we hunger for happiness in life,
God has given us all the good things of life
that we may stay forever young at heart, soaring way overhead like the eagle.

(6) And don't forget all the ways God turns all things to good
and brings justice for people of oppression.
(7) God taught Moses personally about his ways
and led Moses to see his works among his chosen people.
(8) The Lord is full of kindness and grace, patient with us all,
and has more love ready for us than we ever imagine.
(9) He does not chase us down with accusations and blame,
but if he is displeased, he doesn't nurse a grudge.
None of us has gotten what we deserve
or been repaid for the errors of our ways.
(11) "For as high as the heavens are above the earth, so great is his love…
as we learn to reverence and respect him as the Lord.
As far as east is from west, that's how far our God has removed shame from us.
As a father gently loves his children, so the Lord tenderly cares for us as we draw close to him,
especially those who have accepted his covenant of love and love to live by it."
(14) God knows we are fragile creatures made of dust.
Our lives are like the grass—here today, gone tomorrow.
We are as beautiful as a flower today, but a strong wind can take us away,
and we vanish, never to be remembered.
(17) Nevertheless, God's love keeps blessing and sustaining our very existence.
God is continually good to every succeeding generation
as we pass along the faith
and as we keep living God's principles for life.
(19) There is no doubt about the power of his covenant.
We see it reflected in the heavens
and have learned that it stretches throughout eternity.
(20) Let the angels of heaven lead the chorus of praise,
you who live in the mystery of all things
and live in perfect submission to God.
(21) Let all the gathered saints in heaven join in the sweet refrain, all those who live in eternity.
(22) Let everything in creation, everything under God's heaven and earth,
sing the song of praise.
And my very soul will add the voice of utter amazement at the wonder of God my savior.

Psalm 104

For the Beauty of the Earth

(1) O for the greatness of God!
The Lord is wrapped in royal robes of love and majesty. (2) Even the sunny daylight is like his clothing,
while he spreads the heavens out like a canopy (3) and places the footings for them out over the waters.
He makes the clouds his chariot and spreads his wings to ride the winds.
(4) The winds are God's message-bearers; the licking flames of fire are God's house-servants.
(5) God laid the foundations and set the earth upon them.
There it shall stand forever.
(6) God covered her with garments of deep waters, rising high above them all. Then the mountains emerged as God ordered the water to recede. Fearfully, the water backed away as you thundered from heaven, fleeing past the mountains, down into the valleys to your assigned new locations.
(9) There you placed boundaries in your plans for the future, and there within those boundaries they will remain, never again to cover the earth. The springs gush into the ravines, rushing between the mountains.
(11) They water the animals; even the wild animals are so carefully refreshed. The waters provide cool nesting for birds where the birdsongs float among the branches.
(13) Refreshing rains nourish the mountains,
and the earth rejoices in God's provisions.
(14) Grasses grow, plants abound, and all God's creatures find provision. God's people are especially blessed. Wine gives us joy; oil gives us beauty; bread sustains our lives and keeps us healthy.
(16) Trees attest to God's goodness and care;
the loveliest are the cedars of Lebanon.
Birds find homes; storks rest high in the pines.
(18) The rough places have their purpose: mountains for the wild goats, crags for the rabbits.
The moon calculates the seasons for us, and the sun keeps perfect time.
(20) Darkness brings nighttime for resting,
even allowing wild animals to forage.

The lions roar, announcing God's care and their place in the food chain.
The sun quiets them down, and they return for their cool rest from the noonday heat.
Of course, now the way is clear for the people to work until dark creeps back in on little cat feet.
(24) How amazing the way God works his creation plan to perfect timing.
We see God's wisdom throughout the beauty of the earth.
It is teeming with life, and all works according to God's plan.
The sea sings the same song of creation: vast, spacious, full of living things, providing trade routes for us all, while the magic dragon frolics in the sea.
(27) God, you have made it all run like clockwork, every living creature fed right on time.
They eat peacefully right out of your very hand.
When the storms arrive, they know to run for cover. When their life span has run its course,
they become the nourishment of the soil from which they have come.
Your breath gave them life, and they give life to creation!
(31) Lord, your glorious handiwork keeps nourishing us all; may we nourish it in return.
May the cycle of life be pleasing to you, O Lord, for it is created and sustained by your care and made lovely by the touch of your hand.
(33) Lord, you are my song of life; you are my song of joy; you are my song of love; you give your song to me.
(35) One day we who sing of love will outnumber those who grind out the sounds of hate.
May God be praised—may I always praise him.
Let all the earth praise the Lord.

Psalm 105

Blessed Be the Name of the Lord

(1) Oh, be thankful! Call upon the Lord.
Let the nations of the world hear what God has done.
Sing it, tell it, worship, and be confident. God never lets you down.
Call upon the Lord.
(5) Remember this truth. Never let it slip your mind.

Wonders, miracles, acts of justice, a word spoken in time.
Oh, people of God, through the ages God has blessed his covenant people.
He is the Lord and king. He has control of everything.
(8) He keeps his promises to us forever, the word he spoke and kept for a thousand generations,
which he spoke to Abraham and Isaac, confirmed to Jacob as law
and to Israel as an everlasting pledge, saying, "I will give you the promised land as your inheritance."
(12) We were poor, wayfaring strangers, just wandering from land to land.
He carried us and kept his promise. No one could harm, no king oppress.
"Do not touch my special people; do no harm to those who bring the word."
(16) The story of Joseph proved his faithfulness.
God brought famine and sent Joseph, sold as a slave.
They shackled him until he interpreted dreams and brought wisdom
to the foreign king.
From there he became freed and master of the king's household,
ruler of his wealth.
He led his princes and taught his elders wisdom.
(23) When Israel came for help in Egypt, the people lived as strangers.
There, God made them fruitful and numerous yet hated by their captors.
Moses was sent as brother to the king's son; then Aaron also came.
Together they performed signs and wonders there.
(28) God sent darkness because the people were rebellious.
God changed their water to blood; fish, their source of food, died.
The land exploded with frogs infesting their homes and private rooms.
By his voice, God brought swarms of flies and gnats
and turned their rain to hail while lightning terrified them.
(33) As a consequence, further damage came to their food sources—
vines ruined, fig trees sodden, trees downed.
As if that wasn't enough to turn their hearts, God spoke, and further swarms came—locusts, grasshoppers eating everything green. All of their produce was consumed in the pestilence.
(36) Then came the worst and final blow: the firstborn, their prime sign of viral males, these were struck down as well.
Finally, it was enough; Israel was released, and not one declined.

Laden with silver and gold, they marched right out to freedom. Egypt dreaded Israel and their God, so they rejoiced. "Good riddance," the people of Egypt cried as they left.

(39) God again provided, guiding his people with a cloud by day and with fire at night.

God provided quail when they asked, and they called it "the bread of heaven." Water gushed from a rock as God continued to amaze them,

meeting every need.

(43) All this happened because God kept his promise,

the covenant he made with Abraham.

God's people came forth rejoicing; they were his own possession and family, and their joyful

worship distinguished them across the land. That is when he awarded them the inheritance,

the lands of the nations, receiving what had been cultivated by others,

all according to his promise

and their need. (45) They loved God's ways, God's requirements.

"Small price to pay for this glorious care!" they said.

Let all the earth praise the Lord.

Psalm 106

God of Grace, God of Glory

(1) God is so good. Come with thankfulness for all his goodness. He never fails to love us, no matter how far away we wander. The world hungers for those who can tell of God's great works of love. Those who keep his truths and bless those who have been unfairly treated—these are the happiest people on earth.

(4) May my name be on your roster, Lord, when you act to bless your people. I love your works of love, your prospering love, your reclaiming us from the jaws of hell, as you do so often. I want to be in that number when the saints go marching in.

(6) Our record is poor, no better than our predecessors. All of us, like sheep, have wandered aimlessly, even wickedly. When the previous generation gave you the brushoff in Egypt, they just forgot your blessings, your help in time of need. Even while they approached your greatest miracle at the Red Sea, they

stalled faithlessly. Yet you brought them through for the honor of your good name, that Pharaoh's army would know who is in charge.
(9) You spoke the word, and the sun dried up
while you led your people straight through the sands like a desert.
You preserved them from their enemies, from doom and destruction.
Then those bullies were washed away.
Not one survived, while the children of God walked away scot-free and
singing your praises all the way.
(13) But they forgot all that! They were deaf to your calls to trusting faith. It got worse in the desert while they could not delay gratification. They tested you there, O Lord, so you gave in to their whims, gave them what they asked for. Disease set in to teach them the results of such disregard for your helpful guidance. (16) It got worse in the camp. While envy set in, they were jealous of the devotion of Moses and Aaron. What a miracle as the earth opened up and swallowed their two mouthy ringleaders. Then fire consumed those who had swallowed their false lies.
(19) The famous golden calf was erected, and they exchanged their glory for the image of a Wall Street bull!
They had indeed forgotten their God who saved them, whose wonders stunned Egypt and set them free.
God was set to destroy them for such faithlessness, but Moses intervened. The chosen servant of God stayed God's anger. (24) They became ungrateful for the promised land, losing trust in God's faithfulness.
They grumbled in their families; they disobeyed flagrantly. God's anger was white hot by now, and he swore to withdraw his support. They would fall in the desert. Their children would fall out
on the national scene. God would let them wander as they wished,
losing their uniqueness,
overlooking the uniting power of their covenant.
(28) They colluded with the devil; they partnered with folks who did not share their values,
and God's anger was stoked white hot. Sure enough, disease set in.
(30) One righteous man stood up on their behalf, and God listened and relented again,
sending healing powers for all. We can never forget him.
His name was Phinehas.

(32) Still, history repeated itself because they forgot.
At the waters of Meribah, their behavior was so despicable
that Moses lost his cool, screaming, threatening
because of their arrogance in the very face of God's faithfulness.
(34) They had stopped short of the full order of annihilating the pagans and their influence, as the
Lord had commanded. Mingling, they caved in to peer pressure.
They swallowed their empty
traditions of culture and religion. They performed the worst of their
demonic traditions, sacrificing their children whose blood desecrated the
land. This was horrible abomination, and they were doomed. (40) Certainly
now the Lord's anger burned and would consume them. They were so
degraded that their enemies easily captured and enslaved them. God just
handed them over!
(43) How often God had bailed them out, but they were hell-bent on doing
things their own way.
They wasted away in their disregard for God
and their continued wrong choices.
(44) Yet God always heard their cries
as they slipped deeper and deeper in confusion.
God never forgot the pledge, the covenant made between them.
And out of his grace, he shared with them his glory.
Amazingly, every captor pitied them even as they held them captive.
(47) Now here we are, crying again for mercy.
Gather us up that we might sing the sweet songs of salvation once again.
God is the Lord. God deserves all our joy and praise—
all day, every day. If you can agree, then shout your "Amen!"
Let us praise our God for his grace and for his glory.

Book Five

Psalms 107–150

Psalm 107

Because of His Love

(1) Bring your thankful heart to the Lord. Yes, God is good. It is undeniably, powerfully true.
God's love will last forever and ever.
(2) Those who love him, who have found his faithful mercy and grace are sufficient for every need,
they should say what I just said, say it every moment, every day.
(4) So many immigrants sought refuge, wandering, hungry and thirsty, destitute and dying.
They put their hope in the Lord, and he delivered them and brought them through to a new home place.
God is faithful, and these should show their gratitude because his love never fails to see them through.
He is God, the provider, feeding the hungry and slaking their thirst.
(10) Others have experienced depression, prisoners in shackles, wasting away in foreign jails.
Their plight all started with ignorance of God, disregarding God's guidance.
God let them forge out their own pitiful futures, and they fell into disrepute, and there was no one to help.
(13) When they finally cried out to God, he came through for them. He broke the depression,
broke the shackles. They should be thanking God every day for his love. God can deliver.
He is tougher than any jail cells and stronger than any weapons of destruction.
(17) Some others partied so long that they never grew up! They caught hell for their foolishness.
Their fitness plans were so extreme that they nearly wasted away. They, too, cried out to the Lord,
and God came through for them. His word gave them hope, and they were turned around and experienced healing. They should be thanking the Lord for his love. Their gifts of love should be genuine sacrifices, full of gratitude and testimonies of his love with new songs of joy.
(23) Then others grew to be wealthy moguls and merchandizers. They went to sea.

They saw God's wonders at sea. They saw God's power in the storms and faced life-and-death moments at sea,
terrified with every wave of the sea.
(27) Mortified and sickened in the face of God's power of the oceans, they nearly gave up
until they cried out to God and God brought them through.
He stilled the storm to a hush and guided them to safe harbor.
They should be giving thanks for all God's mercies.
Let them tell their stories in the great sanctuaries full of worshipers.
Let them gather the deacons and elders that they, too, can be encouraged.
(33) God is in charge of all of his creation, having the power to change everything by his voice—
the rivers to deserts, the springs to dry ground,
the fertile land to salt flats—because of wicked people there.
God can turn the deserts to pools, the dry ground to springs.
God can bring the hungry to life and help them build thriving communities,
planting fields and vineyards that bring forth lavish harvests.
When God was in their midst, they were fruitful and multiplied, and their herds flourished as well.
(39) In the same way, they experienced humility as their people diminished by oppression,
crises, and sorrow. God can humble the rulers of nations and send them into barren wastelands
in their minds. God will lift the forgotten from their poverty and multiply their families like their flocks.
(42) God's people recognize his hand of blessing and are glad,
but pagans only grumble and complain when things don't go their way.
Let wise people listen to these testimonies
and pay attention to the great love of God.

Psalm 108

The Greatness of God's Love

(1) I have made a commitment never to be broken. Worshiping the Lord is my highest joy.
Wake up, you musicians. Wake up, morning dawn.
(3) I am full of joyful praise, and I want to tell everyone everywhere, singing with all my heart.
(4) My theme is the greatness of your love, higher than the heavens,
and your faithfulness is through the roof.
(5) You always made it happen, Lord, so let's shout it from the rooftops:
"God's people will cover the whole earth!"
(6) O Lord, be our conquering God, that the people you love can make it through their difficulties.
(7) Listen to God speaking through his churches: "In victory I will break up and hand out Asia.
I will measure and set aside the Middle East.
Europe is mine; Africa is mine.
America is my servant; Israel is my crown and scepter.
Russia is my washbasin; on China I toss my sandals.
Over South America I stand up and proclaim our win!"
(10) Whom can I count on to bring me to a safe haven?
Who will lead me to the new place of your favor?
Isn't it you, O God, who has allowed us to decline?
You, Lord, who no longer gives us strength and prominence?
(12) Help us prevail against the pagan nations of violence and corruption, for manmade solutions fail us.
When you stand with us, Lord, we will prevail. The victory is yours.

Psalm 109

O God, I've Had It with These People

(1) O God of my praise, do not be silent, for I have foes like never before, and not a one has regard for the truth.
(2) They have set their minds against anything I try to do,

Book Five: Psalms 107–150

and they spew hatred and spread false propaganda.
How can a ruler get a good job done?
While I had offered them open friendship to work together, they have slandered my motives.
Now they treat me like an outcast, literally like a criminal.
(6) Bring a judge of their own kind to oppose and accuse them.
(7) In the courts let them be found guilty, and let even their own prayers reveal their sinister ways.
(8) The sooner they die off, the better. We need fresh leadership. Replace them.
One stands above the rest. Things cannot be better until he is removed,
his wife a widow,
his children fatherless, his family prominence and home destroyed!
I mean it, Lord, no less!
(11) When the banks seize his assets,
the neighbors overtake his fields and farms,
and when no one volunteers to help him or speak for him,
then he will know what it feels like to be treated the way he has treated me.
I beg you to obliterate him, Lord.
(14) His father was a dishonest, despicable tyrant,
 his mother a shameless hussy.
Don't forget that, Lord, when you finally decide to judge them.
He has not a kind thought in his body
but has been cruel to the poor, the needy, and the broken people.
(17) He cursed others; may he now be cursed! He never gave a blessing; let these be denied him now.
(18) He was distinguished by his cheap phrases of disdain for everyone else.
My prayer is that you, Lord, would give them as good as they have dished out to others.
(21) But do, Lord, do remember me! Help me that I may be a helper and spread your good name.
I know your law is a powerful anchor in my life, so be my helper now.
I have my bad moments, weak as water sometimes.
I get depressed, feeling sorry for myself,
and I wish I could just fade into the woodwork,
be brushed away like a pesky insect.

I punish myself, trying to fast and be purified, but it only serves to make me physically weak.
(25) People have watched me trying to reach up to you, and they laugh and shake their heads.
Strengthen me, Lord, because your love is so strong. Use me as a testimony to your unfailing love.
(26) Others may curse. You will always bless.
When they strike, they will be ashamed, but I will worship all the more.
Their very clothing will be their disgrace and shame.
(30) May my mouth be your instrument of praise and peace,
for you always reach down to the neediest one among us.

Psalm 110

The Lord Provides a Shepherd

(1) Almighty God speaks to our shepherd: "Sit at my place of strength until your foes come to respect you."
God gives strength to our shepherd within his church, and you will prevail!
Your resources await your orders on the day of your victory.
Like a child born in the womb of dawn, you will be exceptional,
fresh as the dew, much beloved.
(4) This is the way God always works, and he never changes.
You are a shepherd from the ancient lines of priesthood.
God will be with you, and his judgments will forever prevail.
He judges all nations with righteousness and truth.
He is nourished by the waters of his creation and therefore will never fail.

Psalm 111

Shout to the Lord

(1) God is so good.
I'm gonna sing when the Spirit says sing…
I'm gonna shout when the Spirit says shout.[1]
God is great and greatly to be praised!
As the congregations gather and reflect intently on all God has done,

how eternal are his works of mercy in our lives,
the world will hear our testimony! How magnificent you are!
(4) The Lord is full of grace and compassion, providing food for those who call in need.
He never forgets his promises.
(6) We have seen his power as he gave the promised land as a home place to his people.
All that the Lord does is just and fair;
all of his life teachings will strengthen us.
(8) His principles are eternal, given to us with love and truth,
keeping us close to him in love.
God makes something wonderful, something good;
all our confusion, he understood.
That's why he provided us with a covenant of love.
Holy and awesome is his name.
(10) "Respect for the Lord is where wisdom finds its beginning."
All who walk in obedience, following him faithfully, will soon come to see clearly how God works in our favor.
"We'll understand it all, by and by."
Praise him; praise.

[1]Line from African-American spiritual "I'm Gonna Sing When the Spirit Says Sing."

Psalm 112

A Good Person, Blessed by the Lord

(1) God is so good!
Happy is the person who trusts in the Lord, who finds wonder and delight in God's ways.
Her children will be strong leaders.
His family, known for their compassion, will be happy.
(3) Prosperity will be their reward,
and being dependably wholesome and good
will be their crown of achievement all of their lives.
Even the dark times will shine with hope and opportunity

for this dependably focused and positive person,
for one filled with grace and mercy,
sharing what they have and known for their selfless service.
When this one is generous and lends their benefits to others,
good will always come of it and be multiplied to him or her.
He is known to be fair to all.
(6) She will be undaunted, whatever life brings.
He will create a legacy of always doing good things.
He is not afraid of bad news because he has set his sights on the good plans and promises of God.
Courage! Trust! Fearlessness! He shall overcome all obstacles.
(9) She is known for sharing her blessings with the disadvantaged.
What a legacy! What an honor!
(10) The doubters who trust in no one but themselves will never understand.
Their jealousy will rage unabashed till they eventually wash away.
All their dreams will end up empty.

Psalm 113

Let the Redeemed Say So

(1) God is so good.
Gather up, everybody. It's time for a camp meeting!
Let's have a "Singspiration," a real time of revival.
(3) Let's keep singing from sunup to sundown.
We can't exhaust the possibilities when we start this heart-warming music.
(4) Our God is the Lord of history, the Lord of all nations, the Lord of heaven.
He watches over all his creation. Whom else have you known who is so faithful and good?
(7) He is concerned for the disadvantaged and makes a way to rise above it all. You watch; God will take the humblest ones and set them among the prominent and the elite.
He even shows his love to the women who have felt forgotten and forlorn.
God provides a home where they find happiness and fulfillment.
That's how good our God is. He never fails. Let the redeemed say so.

Psalm 114
When God Found a Home

(1) When God's people emerged from the slavery of Egypt, God's children from a foreign land,
they became the place where his spirit found a home,
a dwelling place for God!
(3) The oxen ran away at God's voice; the mountains showed their strength; the hills squealed like baby lambs.
(5) Tell me why the waters fled; tell me why the mountains rose; tell me why the hills did sing.
(7) They trembled at the presence of the Lord, descending to find a home among us,
the presence of the almighty.
They remembered that the Lord turned a rock into a pool of refreshment, the rocky mountains into flowing provisions for the people in whom he would dwell.

Psalm 115
It's All About You, Lord

(1) This song is not about us, O Lord—not us, but you. Your love— eternal love—is the theme.
(2) But do you hear the cacophony of dismal doubters?
"Where is their God when they need him?"
Our answer is simple:
"Our God is high above in the heavens, and he moves about freely, sharing his love with his creation."
(3) But they have foolish gods, ones made by their own hands,
made of the very elements of God's own creation,
shaped with mouths that are silent, ears that are deaf, noses that are senseless, hands that are useless, and feet that cannot move.
(8) How foolish. Those who made these gods will be as useless as their gods.
(9) Church, be strong in the Lord. Pastors, be courageous in our God.
Let the people lay hold of their faith with new resolve.
(12) Our God will never forget us nor forsake us.

God will bless his church.
God will bless his pastors.
God will bless his faithful people.
(14) May God be with you and your children and bring you prosperity.
He is God of both heaven and earth.
(16) The heavens are his, but he has given the earth to humankind.
(17) Don't leave it to the past and spiritual heroes of former days
to speak his truth and spread his ways.
(18) It is for us and our generation to pass it on.
It only takes a spark to get a fire going.
God is so good.

Psalm 116

Just Call Me

(1) I love the Lord! How could I do anything else when I realize the Lord heard me calling to him?
I was pleading for mercy when I was up to my neck in alligators.
And because he paid attention as if I was the only person in the world,
I will never hesitate to call on him as long as I live.
(3) I called to the Lord when I was close to death. I knew I was finished.
I could see the grave looming as my next stop.
It grieved me so that I was completely distraught and inconsolable by all who tried to help me.
(4) It is the shortest prayer of all—"Help!"
I was crying out in desperation, "Catch me, Lord. Hold me; never let me go."
(7) What an affirmation of the goodness of the Lord.
He has been good to me, so I calm my very soul with this thought:
Lord, you revived my life, saved me from death, dried my tears,
steadied my feet, led me into your presence again,
brought me home to my people.
(10) Because I trusted that God was able to help me,
I made my cry right up to him:
"I can't make it without you, Lord!"
I realized there was no one else I could trust, not one solitary living soul.
(12) How will I ever repay the Lord for all his goodness to me?

I will hold up that symbol of his love—the wine cup and the bread loaf—
and I will never fail to call out to him.
(14) I will keep every promise I have made to God
and give a testimony to his grace before my church people.
(15) The Lord never overlooks his precious ones
when they are struggling with death.
He sees, he knows, and he loves them all the more.
(16) O Lord, I have seen how great is your love; that's why I am your
servant. You called me; you called my dear mother;
you have kept me free, alive and well.
(17) Please accept my love gift of thanks as an offering to you
as I call upon you again and again.
(18) I say it again: I will keep all of my promises I made to the Lord,
and I will tell my church people every detail of your love.
(19) There is no better place to tell it than among those who also love and
worship you, Lord.
I'll sing praises to his name!

Psalm 117

Praise Him, Praise Him

(1) Praise him, praise him, tell of his excellent greatness.
Let every nation sing. Let all whom God created sing!
(2) His love for us is an everlasting love.
His faithfulness is for all generations of every race and color.
Let's sing praises to his name!

Psalm 118

Unfailing Love

(1) Offer up your thanks to the Lord, for his love is truly good.
His love never fades away.
(2) Let his covenant people confess, "His love never fades away."
(3) Let all of his ministers confess, "His love never fades away."
(4) Let all who love God confess, "His love never fades away."

(5) I cannot forget how he came to set me free
when I was at the end of my rope.
He is always with me. What can any person do to take that from me?
He is always with me. I will hold my head high among those who are
consumed with doubt and fear.
(8) The wise step is to put your trust in God rather than in any person,
or especially in your politics or your national leaders.
(10) I have been threatened by the toughest among them, but they scattered
when I spoke of God's love.
They really pressed me, but they couldn't stand up to the powerful testimony
of God's love.
They swarm like bees but burn up like briars.
(13) There was a time when I couldn't stand up to them,
but God gave me strength.
Here's my motto: (14) "The Lord is my strength and my victory song.
He has set me free time and time again."
(15) Listen to the joyful sound in God's church: "They love to tell the story
of unseen things above."
(17) No, I won't give up. I'll rise up. I'll tell the old, old story of the wonderful
love of God.
(18) Oh yes, there were times of testing, times of God's disciplining me,
but he never gave up on me! He keeps me singing!
(19) Fling wide the church doors for me.
I'm coming to show my thankfulness.
"I was glad when they said unto me, 'Let us go into the house of the Lord!'"
You are all I want, and you are all I need.
(22) The builders cast off what they thought was a damaged stone,
a wounded and imperfect cornerstone.
But in God's eyes, those wounds made the stone a perfect one,
and we have come to understand God's better way.
(24) *This is the day the Lord has made; let us rejoice and be glad in it!*
(25) Lord, give us your peace; give us your prosperity.
Blessed is the one whom God chooses and sends to serve.
We stand with you and send you out with our blessing.
(27) Only the Lord is God, and he has shown us favor.

Let's celebrate!
Let's raise our banners and proceed right up to the church steps.
(28) My God, I love you; I know you are mine.
For you all the follies of sin I resign.
(29) We love you, Lord, and know you are so good. Your love never fails.

Psalm 119 (176 verses)
The A-B-Cs of Faith

(1A) You will be happy if you remain pure. Live by God's laws;
keep ALL God's teachings; seek him with all your heart.
His people never falter, and I wish I were purer in heart.
I would not feel the burden of my past.
Now I will make a fresh start.
Lord, don't give up on me while I strike out on a new course.
(9B) The youth can find purity by studying God's word.
I want this above all things.
I plant your word in my heart that I can BE strong.
Teach me, Lord, for I am ready and hungry for purity.
Let me memorize those special verses that are precious like diamonds.
I wouldn't take a million for them.
As I learn, I grow more and more,
and I am thrilled with what I am learning.
(17C) You may ask God to show you his ways and COUNSEL you.
We need to see to understand things sometimes.
Open our eyes, Lord, the eyes of our understanding!
"We are just pilgrims passing through this world of woe!"
We hunger to know so that we might obey.
We know you reject the proud. The self-sufficient God denies.
Let obedience be some protection for us.
When the rulers of the nations scoff at my faith,
I am strengthened and drawn to your word.
(25D) When you are DOWN and weary, God's word will give you strength.
You have never failed to answer my prayers.
Let me go deeper in your word and understand your ways.
Don't let me slip by with one single deceit.

I'm holding on to your word.
Hold on to me tightly.
(33E) You may ask God to EDUCATE your heart in faith.
Teach me, Lord, how to follow what sometimes seems so hard.
Let me grasp your ways that I may walk in them.
Strip away my selfishness; make me blind to petty things.
Fulfill your promises. Nothing can be more convincing.
I confess my fearfulness. Replace this with your teachings.
(41F) FREEDOM of expression is the gift of being faithful.
I am excited to experience your grace, Lord,
so beautifully promised yet so undeserved.
With grace I can stand up to all the threats,
because your word gives me strength to be faithful.
(43) Don't let your word ever leave my mouth,
because it gives me my only hope.
I love it, trust in it, and will do my best to follow it.
(45) I will walk about in this glorious freedom you give.
I will share your trustworthy word before the highest of the high.
(46) I will speak truth to power, because I have found
it full of real power, and I love it with all my heart.
(48) I lift up holy hands in thanks and prayer.
(49G) God shares his word with you, GIVING you hope when you most.
This is an anchor to my soul in times of storm.
(51) No matter what people may say, I will not relent.
(52) Old memory verses flood into my mind and heart and bring sweet relief.
(53) I feel such righteous indignation at times,
and then I sing the sweet song "Amazing GRACE."
(55) Nighttime brings me quiet to remember your promises,
and that helps me hold them more tightly.
(57H) God is your inheritance, your faithful companion.
I will keep the covenant we have made with all my HEART;
I will always turn to you for guidance
because you promised grace to me always.
(60) Now is the day to grow in grace. There's no time to waste.
I want to make a commitment to face the skies at midnight just
to thank you for the day and remember all you have brought this day,

all the people you brought my way, all the sights of your love in creation.
Stay close to me, and teach me how.
(65I) Learning to follow God's word is something that takes a lifetime.
When we stray, we will always bear the consequences.
I have slipped away and paid a high price!
Returning to obedience is sweet because you will teach me.
(68) When I pay attention to the pure exhilarating power
of your goodness to me, I want to learn more and more.
I take a beating in public sometimes.
Faith can be an ISOLATING character of life, but I play on.
While I am filled with joy, I see the dulling effects of their pride and arrogance.
(71) I can actually attest to the benefits of paying the price for my errors.
I am spurred on to learning more of your word.
It becomes more precious to me by the day,
more precious than a fat bank account and owning all that I want to have.
(73J) You are blessed that you may become a blessing to others.
Lord, you formed me with your own hands.
I will be at my best when you share with me your blueprint for my life.
I want to be a light and a JOY to others who love you,
because your word is alive in me.
Whenever I am down, I hunger to know where I have failed you.
You love never fails—that is what keeps me going!
(77) Don't hold back your tender mercy, because your mercy is what
fuels my motor and keeps me running.
There are many who scoff, but I know the power of your word.
May they have a change of heart.
May I make such an example of the difference your grace makes
that these others may find hope in me. But keep me pure.
(81K) God will KEEP you to the end. His word is his pledge.
When my sight grows dim, straining to see his hands in my life,
when I whine and beg for more, when I become brittle, inflexible
as a wineskin in the smoke, still I will cling to your words of life.
But how long must I wait? I confess my weakness and impatience.
When will you give justice to those who make the way so hard
for those of us who try so hard to do right?
They are relentless, setting traps for us. Help us, Lord, as your word promises.

They would eliminate all of the faithful if they could, but still we persevere.
(88) Let your love keep us till the end,
and we will keep the faith given by your word right to the end.
(89L) God's word LASTS forever!
Written in the heavens, it stands untouched by all else.
(90) God is faithful to every generation, continuously,
and in the creation of the earth,
all God's regular patterns can be seen and trusted.
(91) All God's creation marches to the beat of his eternal word.
I know, because if I hadn't had your word, I would have been lost.
So I can never forget your word. It has been my stronghold.
(94) But don't let go of me, Lord, because I am yours, yours only.
All my troubles wait at my doorstep while I study your word
for its stability, comfort, and safety.
(96) To all our good ideas there is a limit, but your word is eternal.
(97M) MEDITATE on God's word, and your understanding will grow.
Wisdom will come as you study the word of God.
Insights will surprise you and those who teach you and lead you.
Commitment will grow as you study the word of God.
I have not been unfaithful to all you have taught me, Lord.
Your word is sweet, sweeter than honey to my tastes!
As I learn, I discern the wrong path more easily, and I learn to avoid them.
I am learning.
(105N) God's word shines brightest in the NIGHT.
Your word is a guiding lantern for my feet and a lighthouse for my pathway.
I committed my way unto the Lord and confessed
it before my church—that I am yours, Lord. Your word is my sacred duty.
(107) Yes, it has cost me things in life,
but you strengthen my choices by your word.
May the words of my mouth honor you always as you teach me to grow.
I do foolish things so often, but I have never forgotten your word.
(110) There are always those who tempt me,
but I do not stray from the lighted pathway.
Your light is my family heritage, and it gives me joy to follow in their ways.
(112) My heart is yours, and my heart goes on forever.
(113O) God's word will keep you ON track.

(113P) I hate two-faced PEOPLE, and that's why I love your word.
You have always kept me safe when I fully trust your word.
(115S) So SCRAM, teasing tempters! I am keeping faith in the Lord.
Lord, hold on tight, and I'll be able to keep my commitments.
(116T) Stay with me, and I'll make it through the TOUGH times,
because I will not forsake my promises to you.
You stop your help with those who play fast and loose with the truth,
because they're on a dead-end course.
(118U) ULTIMATELY, you let them choose their way.
I am amazed at the way you allow us that freedom,
(120V) But but I am amazed at how foolish we can be, knowing your word never VARIES.
(121W) God knows you belong to him even though you may be WEAK.
Don't let me dangle like a thread in the wind.
Keep me strong and spiritually fit so the fools around me never get a foot in the door.
Sometimes I just go blind, watching for your assured help.
I count on your love when I can't see the results.
I trust your heart when I can't see your hand.
Help me see with my heart when my eyes fail me.
(126X) Hear me, for I think the fools have gone far enough; EXAMINE them.
I implore you to act now.
The more I see your grace, the more I must love what is right
and hate what is wrong.
(129Y) God's word makes you wise and shows you the pathway.
Because YOUR word is so beautiful, I always live by it.
It makes me wise up when I can be so hard-headed.
(131) I hunger for more. Show me mercy as you always do
for those who hunger after what is good.
"Order my steps by your word."[1]
Protect me from wrong. Pull me out of the ditches of life.
Shine the light of your presence on me that I can love and follow your principles of life.
For now I am horrified to tears how this world ignores your word.
(137Z) God is perfect, so all God says is perfect. Be ZEALOUS for it!

God's words are good for us, making us healthy and strong.
My zeal grows thin while I watch the ignorance of so many people.
We have tested and tried and proved your word.
I can't live without every word that proceeds from your mouth.
Every word is perfect, true, eternal.
I have my share of trouble,
but your word always gives me hope and joy and direction.
Your word simply never fails. Lay it on me, Lord!
(145Q) Never QUIT giving your best. Keep your promises.
Call on the Lord. Read and study his word.
Read late at night when you are sleepless. God listens with love.
Hang with me, Lord, because I'm giving it all I've got.
Those closest to me are often those furthest from you.
You are always closer to me.
I learned long ago that I can count on all you say, forever!
(153R) REMEMBER God has the last word when it seems you can't go on.
Sometimes it hurts so bad.
Your compassionate heart, Lord, is your defining character. I count on it.
How can people make it without it?
I catch a lot of flak, but I never surrender.
Idiots surround me, tugging at my sleeve, but I will never resort to less than "fully relying on God!" Sometimes it seems your word is too good to be true,
but every word of yours is a wonderful word of life.
(161S) You will grow STRONG as you stay close to God's word.
Many powerful people the world over claim our faith as weakness,
(162) but we tremble before the power of your word.
Your promises make us happy, like discovering buried treasure.
Loving your word helps us be clearer about what is wrong.
Staying close to you is easy in the scripture because it gives us the
peace that passes all understanding.
(166) Your word builds a holy anticipation in our hearts,
as we are happy to follow on.
Obedience is an exciting challenge.
Finding principles of good living pathways makes us draw close to you,
and we know you see us.
(169) Your tongue is your best tool to offer your love for God.

Hear me, Lord. Teach me, Lord. Give me wisdom, Lord.
Fulfill your promise in me, Lord.
My mouth is overflowing with joyful gratitude.
(172) *O for a thousand tongues to sing my great redeemer's praise.*
The glories of my God and king, the triumphs of his grace.[2]
Help me, Lord. Let me live to praise you that I may thrill to see how you sustain us.
We stray like sheep, Lord. Seek the lost lambs, for we never forget your word.

[1]Line from spiritual folk hymn.

[2]Charles Wesley, "O for a Thousand Tongues to Sing," *Baptist Hymnal* (Nashville: LifeWay Worship, 2008), 136.

Psalm 120

A Person of Peace

(1) Every time I call to the Lord, he answers me.
Don't let my reputation be mistaken or sullied by fools.
God will not tolerate your deception.
Do you not fear what God will do?
He is a warrior when it comes to defending what is true.
He holds the fires of hell for all who are wrong.
I will regret to my dying day this choice to live among a people who
think that war is the way to bring power, that hatred is a way to settle a score.
I am against them and all they stand for.

Psalm 121

My Hope Is in You, Lord

As I look upon the mighty mountains surrounding me, so powerfully created,
I wonder where my own strength comes from.
Clearly, all that I am or ever hope to be comes from the Lord,
who made heaven and earth.
Isn't God powerful enough to keep you from falling?
Yes! He watches over you and never sleeps.
God has kept a vigilant watch over his covenant people, proving that he

never nods, dozes, or sleeps in his care for us!
I am announcing that this God keeps a watch over you personally
and even provides shade from the burning heat of the forces
of angry malice and hatred all through each day.
Neither sun nor moon, nor day or night will ever harm you.
(7) The Lord will guard you from all that threatens to harm you
and all that you fear as he watches faithfully over your life.
The Lord steadies his eyes over you, cradle to grave,
beginning to end, now and always.

Psalm 122

Pray for Peace

I was glad when Sunday finally came and it was time for church.
Everyone was excited about gathering with God's people in God's presence.
So here we are, right in the middle of the holiest place in the world.
Our church is like a city of God, tight, well-directed, fully attentive to God as the center of life.
Right here is where all justice and mercy reign supreme.
(6) Pray for the peace of God's people.
May your people who love God be secure.
May there be peace within your family and safety within your presence.
I will offer to my fellow believers, "The peace of Christ be with you!"
(9) For the sake of all God's people, I will always do my best.

Psalm 123

Keep Your Eyes on the Lord

(1) I will look upon you, Lord, knowing you reign supreme from high above all your creation.
I will look expectantly, fervently as the faithful employee looks to the employer, as a housekeeper looks to the homeowner.
We should look upon the Lord with respect and positive expectation, because God is good to us.
(3) Be kind and gracious—this is what we ask, O Lord.

The world treats us mean, Lord,
and we humbly accept it and turn the other cheek.
(4) Sometimes the rich and famous just wear us out!

Psalm 124
The Right One on Our Side

(1) *Did we in our own strength confide, our striving would be losing;*
Were not the right man on our side, the man of God's own choosing.
The Prince of Darkness grim, we tremble not for him;
His rage we can endure, for lo, his doom is sure:
One little word shall fell him.[1]
Praise to the Lord, who has preserved us.
We have escaped like a bird from the fowler's snare,
and we are free to live another day. (8) *A mighty fortress is our God.*

    [1]Martin Luther, "A Mighty Fortress Is Our God," *Baptist Hymnal* (Nashville: LifeWay Worship, 2008), 656.

Psalm 125
What a Mighty God We Serve

(1) God makes persons strong as the mountains, mighty, unshaken, and lasting forever.
The Lord surrounds us like the mountain rim around the valley.
He has given us this land as a safe haven. All threats are only temporary taunts.
(4) Lord, show us what you alone can do
for those who place their trust in you.
But those who break stride and run in cowardice,
they will receive a coward's reward.
God's people love peace, and they shall have it!

Psalm 126

Homecoming

(1) When the Lord brought us back to his safety and presence,
we could hardly believe it.
It was a dream come true. We were hilariously joyful, singing all the way.
The surrounding nations saw it all and were duly impressed.
They, too, sang "Amazing Grace." All those pagan peoples claimed the great hymns for themselves too.
(3) Truly, God has acted mightily for us, and we are humbly grateful.
Let the rivers of mercy and the floodtides of fortunes cut loose again for your people, Lord.
Let the tears of our mothers be like seeds planted to bring forth a harvest of great praise and joy.
(6) Now we believe. The people who go courageously into their troubles
and carry their hopes like a breadcrumb trail
will surely return for homecoming, their bounty with them.

Psalm 127

The Excitement Is Building

(1) Unless the Lord has given the order and the blueprint, we all build our lives in vain.
Unless the Lord is invited as your guardian and keeper, all your efforts at insurance are in vain.
(2) Work hard as you may, crack of dawn to the wee hours, struggling to accumulate your future.
It's all in vain. The Lord gives peaceful sleep to those who walk every day in his love.
Children are our heritage, a reward and a trust.
They are our little weapons against the threats of an uncertain and uneasy future for our land.
We are blessed when God fills our churches with wonderful children.
They will be well prepared for anything the tough future may throw at us!

Psalm 128
Trust and Obey

(1) *When we walk with the Lord, in the light of his word, what a glory he sheds on our way.*[1]
We enjoy the blessing of hard work.
Our family prospers and is as productive as a garden.
Our children have boundless energy and enjoy life.
Trust and obey, for there's no other way to be happy each day.
May God bless you among his people every day of your life.
May you live to see God's church prevail, and may you live long in the land God gave you,
long enough to share the joys of grandchildren.

[1]John H. Sammis, "Trust and Obey," *Baptist Hymnal* (Nashville: LifeWay Worship, 2008), 500.

Psalm 129
A Motherless Child

(1) *Sometimes I feel like a motherless child, a long way from home.*[1]
But my troubles have never done me in!
(3) I feel like a field of produce, harrowed, turned under, plowed up in the farmer's land,
but you, Lord, have never yet let me down.
(5) May all the enemies of God be exposed and shamed,
withering like flimsy weeds
growing in the gutters of your rooftop.
They never amount to all they promise, nor is there enough substance to fill a wheelbarrow.
(8) Never settle for the meaningless well-wishing of people
who pass by but never stop to understand or stop to offer help.

[1]Line from a spiritual folk hymn sung by Odetta, "Sometimes I Feel Like a Motherless Child."

Psalm 130

Out of My Bondage

(1) *Out of my bondage, sorrow and shame, Father, I come; Father, I come.*[1]
My plea is for mercy, Father.
If you held our wrongs against us like we do others,
there would be no hope for any of us. But your grace and mercy give us hope and a tomorrow.
(5) I will be patient, Lord.
Deep inside I will wait as I find strength in your word.
(6) I will be as vigilant as the ancient watchman on the wall
waiting for the dawn, the precious sight of first light.
(7) Church, refocus your hope in the Lord rather than all your earthly signs of success.
With God's love, you can move mountains again.
You can do the impossible, completely unhindered by past mistakes, griefs, or heartaches.
(8) God washes us all white as snow.

[1] William T. Sleeper, "Jesus, I Come," *Baptist Hymnal* (Nashville: LifeWay Worship, 2008), 439.

Psalm 131

Pour Contempt on All My Pride

(1) *Were the whole realm of nature mine, that were a present far too small.*[1]
I will not question this love so amazing, so divine,
but I am content like a child at its mother's breast.
Like a child ready to stand and walk, I am quiet, studying myself, ready for a first step.
Church, God's faithful are good. Let go of small worries, and let God take the reins, now and always.

[1] Isaac Watts, "When I Survey the Wondrous Cross," *Baptist Hymnal* (Nashville: LifeWay Worship, 2008), 234.

Psalm 132

I Love Thy Kingdom, Lord

(1) O Lord, when David was a man after your own heart,
he made a vow and took a step to secure the kingdom for you.
His oath to you was one for the ages, made through hard-fought battles and
unbending commitment.
(2) This is what he swore unto you that day:
"I will not sleep or take comfort in my own place.
I will not allow rest to comfort my own weariness
until I find a place for the Lord, the place of thine abode."
(6) It has been our theme throughout our journey,
from battlefields to farm land:
"Let us find sanctuary in God's house.
Let us bow before him at his chosen altar."
(8) Arise, Lord, and come to your kingdom places, you and all the joys
of remembrances.
Let our ministers stand before us as shining examples.
Let all the saints lead us in the "Hallelujah" chorus.
(10) Let the legacy of David, the shepherd and the king,
be proudly remembered.
Let your covenant with David be remembered, Lord,
the one promise that provides leadership for generations to come
if our children keep the covenant and we teach God's life principles.
This is your promise for our heritage and for all generations.
(13) Lord, you expressed your choice of the kingdom,
and you expressed your pleasure for the place for your presence:
(14) "This is my place, my throne, my heart's desire, my place of provisions
and blessings.
I will care for the poor. I will fill my ministers with every need
and songs of joy for my precious and chosen people."
David has shown his spirit—it's right! I will provide for every need of his
spirit and set an eternal flame.
But for those who mock my rightful place, I will cover them with shame.
David's crown will amaze the world. "This is my place, my kingdom!"

Psalm 133

How Sweet It Is

(1) The mutual respect that produces our sense of community and brotherhood—this unity is so sweet!
It is like the sweet perfume from my father's hair and beard,
streaming down his face and over his jacket as he holds me close.
(3) It is as if the morning dews of our mountaintop climb
were dropping down upon us in the hills below,
for in this unity is where we find God's presence and his richest blessings.

Psalm 134

I Love the Lord

(1) Lift up your voices, all you ministers and followers of our God,
those who keep the doors open and the lights burning in God's house.
(2) Raise your hands in joyful worship in his sanctuary,
and sing with a confident heart.
(3) Now may the great God of the universe, the God who hears us,
pour out strength, wisdom, and respect to you from his church people.

Psalm 135

Sing Praises to His Name

(1) God is so good.
(2) Speak up about God's goodness, all of you who have received grace upon grace and all of you
who have been given a call to serve him and his people in the place where God is at home in our hearts.
(3) God's good news cannot be suppressed, so let's tell the world.
Sing songs of happiness in the Lord.
(4) God made a choice to let his spirit rest upon a people who would faithfully bear it to the world,
and we are his, the sheep of his pasture, a treasured possession.
(5) I have experienced God's greatness, greater than all the things we falsely put our hopes in.

(6) God is sovereign in all the heavens,
in every corner of the earth, and in all the seas.
(7) God rules the clouds, the rain and lightning, the winds and the weather.
(8) You should have seen how he dealt with the Egyptian people,
whose leader tried to stand against God's plans.
He struck down the treasured firstborn of people and animals.
He sent signs and wonders into the land,
all to teach Pharaoh an important lesson about his sovereignty!
(10) He dealt with many nations and mighty kings who challenged his authority over creation,
and he gave away their lands to the people who would be faithful.
(13) That's why we sing. His power is made perfect in our weakness.
His peace passes all understanding.
His mercy is so good, so precious, so readily available to all who would be faithful to him.
(15) Our possessions of things we value
are only the crafts made at our own hands.
We may shape mouths for them, but they cannot speak;
eyes, but they cannot see;
ears, but they cannot hear; lungs,
but they cannot breathe.
And the irony is that all who worship their possessions
become as dead and lifeless and useless as their things.
(19) Let this be a lesson to all of us in God's church family.
When we sing praises to his name, we encourage and bless each other
and build up each other's faith. Let the church rise up singing.
Let our songs tell about the God who lives within us!

Psalm 136

A Litany for God's Forever Love

(1) Let's be thankful, for God never fails.
People: God's love goes on forever.
Let's be thankful, for God is above everything in worship.
People: God's love goes on forever.
Let's be thankful, for our God is at the heart of all creation.

People: God's love goes on forever.
(4) To God above, who can make all things possible.
People: God's love goes on forever.
By his wisdom, God created the heavens above.
People: God's love goes on forever.
(6) Who spread out the earth upon the seas.
People: God's love goes on forever.
(7) Who created light to sustain all of life.
People: God's love goes on forever.
(9) The moon and the stars reign in the skies all night.
People: God's love goes on forever.
(10) To him who taught a lesson in power and truth to the enemies.
People: God's love goes on forever.
And preserved his covenant people in the midst of disaster.
People: God's love goes on forever.
(12) And with a mighty hand, God performed his plan.
People: God's love goes on forever.
(13) To him who astonished the world by dividing the Red Sea.
People: God's love goes on forever.
And tenderly led his people right through it over dry land.
People: God's love goes on forever.
(15) But swept the foolish, evil Pharaoh right out into the waters.
People: God's love goes on forever.
(16) To him whose leading hand guided us through deserts.
People: God's love goes on forever.
And overthrew great kings who threatened us.
People: God's love goes on forever.
Whom we can name one by one.
People: God's love goes on forever.
(21) And gave their land to us as an inheritance, to us, his own people.
People: God's love goes on forever.
(23) To the God who saves us in distress and broken-heartedness.
People: God's love goes on forever.
And came to set us free.
People: God's love goes on forever.
Who feeds every living creature.

People: God's love goes on forever.
Oh, yes! Let's be thankful, for the God of all creation never fails us.
People: God's love goes on forever.

Psalm 137

Sweet Homeland

(1) On the banks of the Euphrates River in Babylon,
we wept as we remembered the people and places of home.
On the branches of the poplar trees, we hung up our guitars,
for there our enemies asked for our songs of home.
Those who tormented us demanded that we sing joyfully,
like the songs we are known for from home.
(4) But how can we sing with broken hearts and disappointed dreams in a foreign land?
(5) Oh, homeland! If we ever forget our peaceful places,
may our hands deny the art that reflects you;
may our tongues stick to the roof of our mouths if I forget you, my homeland!
(7) Lord, remember those days when our tormentors
shamed and taunted our faithand our sacred places, saying,
"Tear it down! All the way to its foundations!"
O pagan people, terrorists, destroyers of the faith, you are doomed to be erased and forgotten,
and so proud will be the armies that bring you down for what you have done to the people of God.
These ones will carry out the will of God thoroughly.

Psalm 138

Great Is Thy Faithfulness

(1) When I sing my songs of praise,
I will sing with a joyful and confident heart
for all the world to hear, because you, O Lord, have done such lovely things,
far above what we can imagine.
(3) You answered my prayers and made me courageous.
(4) I'd like to teach the world to sing your song in perfect harmony,

to sing the songs I know by heart that tell the strength you gave to me.
(6) Though you are mighty, you care for the lowly, but from the haughty you keep your distance.
(7) Though I walk through the valley of the shadow of death,
you are always with me, extending your arms of love and protection.
(8) It is just what you said you would do, and I have seen your faithfulness over and over.
You never cease to amaze me. Please never stop your faithful care.

Psalm 139

The Everlasting Arms

(1) *O Lord, you know me; you know my thoughts.*
You light the path before my way.[1]
You know my every thought.
You are watching and waiting with me in every move I make.
(4) Before I speak, you understand my words and speech.
(6) When I stop to think of all this, it is too wonderful,
too high for me to comprehend.
(7) Where can I go from your presence?
Where can I escape your watch, your eyes, your ears, your heart?
Should I run to the skies, you would be there. You made them.
If I laid down in the gutter, behold, you are there.
If I dream dreams at dawn or if I should flee to an island retreat,
even there your hands would spread a path before me.
Your capable hands never let go.
(11) If I should think to hide like a child in the dark,
or if in discouragement I let the low feelings of dark days swallow me,
your light will find a way to shine through the darkness.
For the darkness will only be as light when you are there.
(13) All this is true as you created my inward self.
You are Creator God, who knit the tissues of my body in my mother's womb.
(14) I am in awe of your wonderful ways to create my life, any life.
I am a true believer.
(15) No random selection occurred under your nose, though it was hidden from our naked eyes.

You watched my creation; you saw it all.
You planned my time on earth,
numbering all my days as if you kept a captain's log.
You wrote them down ahead of time.
(17) I value every one of these thoughts, O Lord, and at the countless volume of your thoughts,
I marvel and cherish them every one.
If I were counting, it would be like the grains of sand on the seashore.
Then, aha! I awaken, and you are still here with me.
(19) What I do not understand is how you allow the evil in this world.
If you would only strike them down!
I reject them and want to run them off.
They disrespect you; they are malicious;
they pretend to use your name as their reason to stir up trouble.
(21) Surely you can see how deeply I hate those who show no regard for you, O Lord.
I will not give them the time of day. They truly are enemies.
(23) But I must let you examine my own heart, my motives.
Try me, too, Lord, because my own anxiety rises deep within me.
I would give up anything that offends you, Lord.
Lead me, Lord. Lead me in your perfect ways.

[1]Line from Bill and Linda Cates, "Hal's Song (Psalm 139)," Recording: *The Greatest of These*.

Psalm 140

Hear Our Prayer, O Lord

(1) Rescue me! Take me in your arms! Rescue me!
Protect me from violent persons who scheme and plan and disturb the peace of the nations.
(3) Their rhetoric creates doubt and suspicion; their sedition poisons us
and erodes the trust we have built between us.
(4) Build a wall around me. Guide my steps,
for their plans are devious and dangerous; their pride is a silent killer.
Like tripwires set for the peacekeepers, they have booby-trapped the landscape.

(6) But I will hold my head high and proclaim that you are God.
You are greater than the world's alarms.
Hear our prayer, O Lord! Be merciful!
(7) You are the God of all the earth, and you are my Savior God,
protecting me when I face conflict.
Don't give them an inch, O Lord,
those who pretend to have a legitimate cause.
They are pretending, and any quarter you allow them will lead to selfish pride.
(9) They have tormented me; let the same fall upon them.
(10) May the fires of hell lick their heels until they sink deep in the mess
they have caused.
We have no time to deal with them.
This land is full of people who would kill their own family just to get ahead.
Let them feel the heat of their own violence.
(12) Lord, you have taught us that fair treatment
and compassion for the least fortunate among us is the way of life.
You fight for them, and so should we.
(13) Good and decent people know
where this impulse of compassion comes from,
and they live in joyful praise of your heart, our creator and redeemer.

Psalm 141

Take Time to Be Holy

(1) I am calling, Lord, calling like a priest at the altar,
asking for your purifying work in my life.
(3) First of all, Lord, give your protective covering for my mouth, for I tend to have loose lips.
Guard my heart from even thinking of wrong,
especially sharing in the plentiful and tempting shortcuts all around me.
(5) Lord, send a friend, a good person, someone to mentor me,
a companion to walk with me and hold me accountable.
Mostly I pray against the delicious schemes of deceit all around me
and against those who live them. Back me up, Lord.
Let some of these see the error of their ways
by what I profess to live and believe.

(7) They will remember the testimony of your judgments of the past,
and they will be amazed and encouraged to change.
(8) Lord, as I keep my eyes on you, I, too, remember your power and love,
your justice, and I find my hope and strength in you. Hold me close to you.
Protect me.
(10) As I walk in my daily commitments to you,
take out those who mock you,
and let them fall victim to their own foolish ways.

Psalm 142

Standing in the Need of Prayer

(1) *Sweet hour of prayer, sweet hour of prayer, that calls me from a world of care.*[1]
(3) I will list out my troubles before you,
because I know you are the one who cares and is always with me and listening.
You know I am besieged by the people who would bring me down.
Among those who profess such loyal friendship,
there is not one who really understands or truly cares.
(5) But it is different with you, Lord. My lifelong cry is this:
You alone are my heart's desire, and I long to worship you.
You alone are my strength and shield; to you alone may my spirit yield.
(6) In desperation I cry.
It is an imprisonment, as I know the enemy is too strong for me.
Unlock the gate and set me free
that I might sing the sweet, sweet song of salvation.
The congregation will gather up with me to hear the songs I sing of your
unfailing goodness.

[1]William Walford, "Sweet Hour of Prayer," *Baptist Hymnal* (Nashville: LifeWay Worship, 2008), 429.

Psalm 143

My Faith Looks Up to Thee

(1) As I cry again for mercy, I know my unworthiness, and I know your love and faithfulness.
Come to me now.
(2) Withhold your judgment, because though we all deserve it, none of us could bear it.
(3) This is about the loneliness of doing right and following your way.
We feel crushed and shoved into dark corners,
worthless in the face of such surrounding greed and arrogance.
The spirit is willing, but the flesh is weak.
(5) I think of better days, of the good times, and I thrill to the memory of the stories of past days of wonder.
How naturally I reach up again to you from those days. It's a desert reaching up for your refreshing rains.
(7) I don't know how long I can last, so I plead for your ever-present help.
I plead just to see your power displayed, or I will sink like a rock.
(8) May tomorrow be better and bring me hope, for my faith looks up to you.
Show me the path that leads to life.
Snatch me from the jaws of hate.
Teach me how to grasp the anchor that holds.
You alone are God. Your Spirit can sustain me.
(11) I ask my prayer for your own sake, Lord.
Save me that I may serve you.
You are too good to let your own character be doubted.
This is your servant praying. They are your enemies, as they are mine.
Let it stop.

Psalm 144

A Mighty Fortress

(1) *A mighty fortress is our God—a bulwark never failing.*[1]
Strength! Deliverance! You train me for conflict.
You coach me about the evils of this world.
You ready me to do battle with wrong.

(3) We are only a tiny speck in your vast creation, yet you see and care for us!
Our lives are frail; every generation holds on with a breath and a prayer.
(5) Split the skies and descend, O Lord.
Touch the mountains and let them rumble and explode.
Send lightning and thunder on the armies of shame.
(7) Enemy nations can never understand your grace,
and their deception hides the truths
you have given us so we might live abundantly.
(9) But I have a new song to you, O Lord.
On my guitar I'll sing a song of your mighty power,
power available to all who choose what is right,
power you gave to the servant of your people long ago.
(11) Do it again, O Lord; set me free.
Lift me like a city on a hill above the nations that do not accept your grace
and whose deception is deadly.
(12) Then our children will flourish like greenhouse plants—
sons like tall trees, daughters like columns in the palace, hand carved in beauty.
Then our barns will be full of the harvest,
our herds increasing by thousands in our fields,
(14) our merchants strong, our industry brilliant and powerful.
No one will copy our genius, none enslaving us to their technology,
no poverty, none left behind in our prosperity.
(15) We are blessed, blessed all because our God is the Lord,
the creator, sustainer, redeemer of all living things.

[1]Martin Luther, "A Mighty Fortress Is Our God," *Baptist Hymnal* (Nashville: LifeWay Worship, 2008), 656.

Psalm 145

O Worship the King

(1) *O worship the king, all glorious above, and gratefully sing his wonderful love.*
Our shield and defender, the Ancient of Days,
pavilioned in splendor and girded with praise.
(4) *O tell of his might, O sing of his grace,*
whose robe is the light, whose canopy space.

(7) *Thy bountiful care what tongue can recite?*
It breathes in the air, it shines in the light.
(8) *Thy mercies how tender, how firm to the end,*
*Our Maker, Defender, Redeemer and Friend.*1
(9) Lord, you are full of grace and compassion
for all you have created.
And all of your creation will praise you.
Especially will your own people be filled with love for you,
telling the stories of the kingdom where and when you reign and rule.
They will tell it so all people will know your grace is enough
for every need we have,
and your kingdom will be forever and forever, your power throughout the universe displayed.
(13) Lord, you are faithfully dependable to all you have spoken to us,
your people.
You are yet more; you are loving to all and careful to care for those who have been left behind.
(15) All creation is dependent upon you, and you never fail,
feeding them all right when they need it.
The resources of life are in your hands, and you satisfy all living things.
(17) How great is our God—pure and perfect,
holy and full of grace to all of creation.
The Lord is very close to all who reach up to call on him—
all who call with sincerity and in genuine humility and put their trust in you.
(19) He fills the hearts of those who hunger for him.
He hears their genuine prayers of faith, and he answers every one.
(20) The Lord watches with care those who love him,
but those bent on their selfish ways will find him far away when they need him most.
(21) *"I am thine, O Lord; I have heard thy voice, and it told thy love to me.*
*But I long to rise in the arms of faith and be closer drawn to thee."*2
Let's all lift our voices in joyful praise!

[1]Robert Grant, "O Worship the King," *Baptist Hymnal* (Nashville: LifeWay Worship, 2008), 24.

[2]Fanny Crosby, "I Am Thine, O Lord," *Baptist Hymnal* (Nashville: Life Way Worship, 2008), 535.

Psalm 146

Our God Reigns

(1) *Let's just praise the Lord, praise the Lord.*
Let's just lift our hands toward heaven and praise the Lord.[1]
(3) Don't put your ultimate trust in those whose lives are as short as your own.
What can mortal persons do to give you life?
When they die, their bodies are buried in the grave just like your own,
and their thoughts and plans are buried with them.
(5) But those who trust God for life, who hope in all God's promises,
the great God of heaven and earth, the faithful-to-the-end God,
they will always be confident and at peace.
(7) He cares for the broken people and the hungry people.
He sets free the falsely accused.
He gives eyes to the blind that they may see.
He lifts the downhearted. He loves those who do good.
He guides those who immigrate for a better chance at life.
He is the one who gives real life and joy to abandoned children
and to lonely women and widows.
He confounds the ones who are set to build their world and their wealth on
the backs of these.
The Lord is God forever—
he reigns over all generations of people, and we can see it among his people.
Let's be grateful and joyful in the Lord.

[1] Line from Gloria Gaither and William J. Gaither, "Let's Just Praise the Lord," *Baptist Hymnal* (Nashville: LifeWay Worship, 2008), 145.

Psalm 147

Praise Him, Praise Him

(1) Nothing lifts our hearts like the songs of great joy to our God.
These songs build our faith and give us confident hope.
So let's just praise the Lord!
(2) The Lord builds his church.
God gathers those who have been scattered away from their homes.
The Lord heals those whose dreams have been crushed and disappointed,

and God binds up their wounded hearts.
(4) God counts the stars, naming them one by one.
(5) God reaches out to those who are sincere
and brings the prideful to their knees.
(7) Sing, everyone! Raise a song of thanksgiving!
Make music on every instrument available, and lift that song up to our God.
(8) Our Creator God has provided clouds to bring rain from the heavens,
refreshing the earth, making grass to cover the lush green hillsides.
God is feeding our cattle and the birds of the air.
What a perfect plan of provision.
(10) But understand God's heart—
all of this is to provide a heart for God's people—
respect, trust, hope, and lives built on love.
It's not the power we so often claim is everything.
Trust not in powerful horses and strong bodies, but hearts strong enough to love like God loves.
(12) This is whom we worship and offer our songs of joyful praise,
for God lives among the community God creates.
(14) It is God who gives peace to your bodies, not walls.
It is God who makes your crops excel, whose word grows in excellence and covers the earth.
(16) Look again at God's plan of creation.
Snow blankets the earth like a woolen shroud. Frost dots the land like ashes.
Hail pounds down like pebbles.
Who can withstand his icy blast of judgments that cleanse and purge the land?
(18) But he sends God's word and melts it all, sending gentle breezes and flowing waters.
God has made clear his word to his people,
and God's laws and life principles are ready for our healthy living.
But no other peoples have been given so much,
and they also do not have God's instruction, or boundaries, or way of life.
How can we keep from singing?

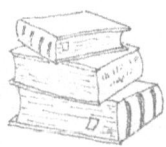

Psalm 148

I Stand Amazed

(1) Bless you, O Lord! Let the heavens shout your praises—
angels in heaven, a host of heaven's choirs,
sun and moons, stars above, the Milky Way,
and all the constellations beyond it.
Let them all shout the name of the Lord, because he made them every one
by speaking their names!
He placed them carefully above,
and his word never fails to accomplish his purposes.
(7) Let the seas cough up their contents,
every creature in the ocean deeps singing about the wonders of their creator.
Let the weather in every season tell the tale of the one who made them—
lightning, hail, snow, clouds, storms, and wind that follow God's plans.
Mountains and hills, fruit trees and mighty cedars,
wild animals and cattle herds,
scurrying creatures and flying birds, kings and politicians, high and low,
young men and girls, old men, ladies, and children—
(13) let them all glory in the wonder of their creator,
who is high above all things he created, higher and more lofty than the skies,
the earth, the plants, and the constellations.
(14) God has a plan. God will provide for all his creation.
God gives us voices to sing glory to his wonderful love.
God gives his people a song.
I stand amazed in the presence of the one who draws us close to his heart.
God is gracious!

Psalm 149

I'll Live for Him

(1) Let's sing about God's goodness!
Find the new song in your heart,
and bring it for all the congregation to join in.
(2) Let the people of God, chosen to bear his light to the world, sing it.

Let them dance, and let the orchestra play—all of it unto the Lord,
giving pleasure both ways.
(4) For the Lord delights in his people,
reaching forth to the lowliest to lift them high and set them free to find more life in him.
(5) Let our leaders, revered and respected, find joy in their restricted age,
in their convalescence and in retirement. O be joyful!
(6) May their mouths be filled with joyful stories,
telling of God's blessings through their lifetimes.
And may these testimonies be sharp as a two-edged sword,
separating truth from deception, good from evil,
honest effort from greedy ambition.
May these testimonies reveal the rulers who have stolen from their people and robbed God.
(9) Why this truth is told? This is the glory of God's people.
I'll live for him, and I invite us all to join in the sweet songs of salvation.

Psalm 150

Let All the World in Every Corner Sing

(1) Let's sing about God's goodness!
Let the church people sing like the angels in heaven,
praising him throughout the skies.
(2) We shall praise him for all he has done in love for his people
and praise him for the great scope of his loving kindness.
(3) Pull out the trumpets, and let them blare aloud.
Tune up the strings, harps, violins, guitars.
(4) As we dance, the tambourines will give us rhythm.
Joyfully we will praise God with gentle flutes and clashing cymbals.
Then do it all again, letting your hearts be filled with joyful exaltation.
(6) Let everything that has breath join in the excitement,
the inspiration, the praise of our God for his goodness to us.

Writer's Note

As a pastor of a lifetime of ministry, I must insist that worshiping God is the key to a growing faith, one that must grow or die. There are signs that evidence of such familiar faith is dwindling away today to be replaced by all the seemingly more important day-to-day, practical aspects that every one of us faces. And our very lives demand an alert and relevant grasp on every twist and turn of our culture, our world, and our personal lives. We all believe in something, and worshiping God can be the key to the relevance of a living, growing faith in God for each of us.

Faith in God's living presence in our lives is the genius of the Hebrew faith, handed down to us through the Old Testament scriptures. Our personal faith is our relationship with this ever-present God. It is the essential relationship, and like any others we enjoy, it either is nurtured by regular and active contact, shared hours, great moments, days of reflection and appreciation of our intertwining lives, or it soon is found to be essentially irrelevant. We move on.

But as a life source, worship is essential to our faith relationship. Worship as offered through the psalms strengthens the resolve, eases the tensions, instructs the mind, and enlarges the heart.

If these sound like tired phrases of "church-ology," I heartily understand. I grew up as a PK, a "preacher's kid"! My life was consumed with church life, church people, and the church "program" was the answer to all the needs of our home life. In fact, sometimes the individuals of our family seemed swallowed up in the great and grand scheme of our church experience. It was only as I grew into manhood that I began to understand and appreciate the masterful recipe of church as a builder of the greatest individuality—life abundant, as Jesus called it—character, and opportunity.

In church, relationships abound. Learning is at the core. Perspectives are examined, massaged, and choices are thrust upon you in ever increasing measure. John I Durham, scholar of The Psalms, once preached of a church sign on the highway that read, "CAUTION, CHURCH!"

We do, however, take ourselves a little too seriously when we equate belonging to a church with salvation itself. It was, as Brian McLaren wrote, "an experience in missing the point!" Church is a place where we learn of God and are led into and enabled to worship.

When we worship, we grow, experience God, and become fully alive. The psalms are the Hebrew songs that Jesus knew, and they have become the means by which we, too, may draw close to God, where we can learn to be honest *with* and *about* God. These renditions gushed forth from my mind and heart after finishing 45 years of shepherding the flock of the Good Shepherd. These are fresh words inspired by my love for and use of the psalms . Few things stir my faith like the psalms. I offer them to you for the same experience.

WGH

Psalms, Catalogue of Purposes, Suggested Use

The 33 Most Familiar Psalms: Praise and Lament

(1) Blessed is the man...Affirmation
(2) Why do the nations...Affirmation
(8) What is man...Affirmation/Praise
(11) If the foundations are destroyed...Affirmation/Praise
(19) The heavens are telling...Affirmation/Praise
(22) Why hast thou forsaken me...Cry for Faith
(23) The Lord is my shepherd...Affirmation/Poem/Devotional
(24) The earth is the Lord's...Affirmation/Call to Worship
(27) The Lord is my light...Affirmation/Testimonial
(34) O taste and see...Affirmation/Testimonial
(37) Commit your way...Testimonial/Call to Worship
(42) As a hart longs...Cry for Hope
(46) God is our refuge and strength...Affirmation/Devotional
(48) Great is the Lord...Affirmation/Call to Worship
(51) Create in me a clean heart...Cry/Confession
(84) How lovely is thy dwelling place...Affirmation/Devotional
(90) Thou hast been our dwelling place....Devotional/Prayer
(91) He who dwells in the shelter...Affirmation/Testimonial
(95) Harden not your hearts...Call to Worship
(96) O sing to the Lord a new song...Call to Worship
(100) Make a joyful noise...Call to Worship
(103) Bless the Lord, O my soul...Prayer/Call to Worship
(111) The fear of the Lord is the beginning...Praise
(116) Precious in the sight of the Lord...Meditation/Devotional
(118) This is the day the Lord has made...Liturgical Testimony
(119) Thy word is a lamp...(longest psalm) Instruction/Commitment
(121) I will lift up mine eyes unto the hills...Affirmation/Call to Worship
(122) I was glad when they said unto me...Call to Worship
(127) Unless the Lord builds the house...Call to Worshipful Retreat

(133) Behold how good and pleasant.....Call to Worshipful Retreat
(137) By the waters of Babylon...Cry/Lament
(139) Where can I go from thy Spirit...Personal Devotional
(145) Great is the Lord and greatly to be...Praise

Liturgical Calls for Offerings and Sacrifice

(38) An offering of repentance and sacrifice
(50) A sacrifice of thanksgiving
(70) An offering for God's help
(100) An offering of thanksgiving
(116) An offering of worship

Psalms of Litanies of Historical Accounts

(54) A deceitful neighboring ally
(55) A deceitful friend
(57) The threat of distrustful cohorts
(59) Discovering an enemy
(63) When alone, lonely
(70) Discovering religious misunderstanding
(78) A history of God with his people

www.ingramcontent.com/pod-product-compliance
Lightning Source LLC
Chambersburg PA
CBHW070938180426
43192CB00039B/2330